Locket's Meadow

The Long Road Home

By
Kathleen M. Schurman

Illustrations By
Catherine W. Hamill

ISBN: 1-4140-4890-4 (e-book)
ISBN: 1-4140-4889-0 (Paperback)

Printed in the United States of America
Bloomington, IN

This book is printed on acid free paper.

1st Books - rev. 01/21/04

For my family, David, Matt and Bo, who are
also my very best friends –
my life is filled with magic, and so much of it is
because of you – my love for you is eternal.

Locket's

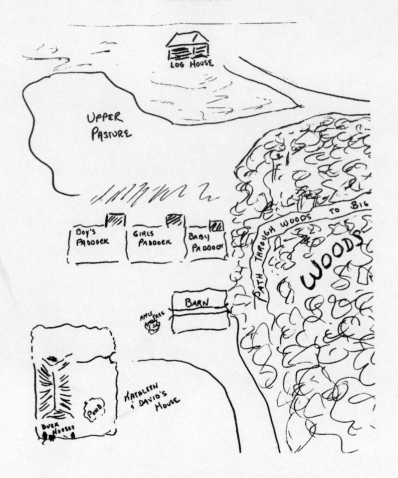

Meadow

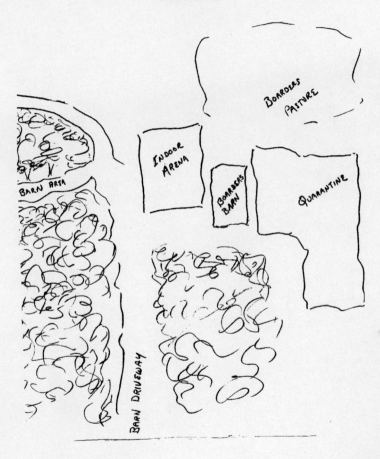

Chapter One

The house that spews food

A young crow named Wilson was on the move early one August day. He'd gotten into a scuffle with a red-tailed hawk over who would get to sit on a certain fence post and it had turned ugly, so he'd decided to move along and find a new place to hang out for a while.

Wilson soared over a large pond surrounded by fields of daisies, black-eyed Susans and brown and white cows. He thought about stopping for a rest, but then he spotted a tall pine tree a short distance away with a small flock of crows crowded onto its lower branches. Beneath the tree sat a little white farm house, several barns and pastures dotted with horses. It looked friendly enough, and he decided to drop in and introduce himself to the neighborhood.

He flew in and landed between two other crows, neither of whom took much notice of him.

"Dudes! Wassup?" Wilson asked.

"Waiting," one of them replied, not moving his eyes from the back door of the little white farm house below the towering pine.

Wilson followed the crow's gaze and watched the back door for a few seconds.

"What are we waiting for?" he asked.

"The house is going to start spewing food soon," the other crow replied.

"Spewing?" Wilson looked at the door with alarm. "What do you mean, spewing?"

The crow on the other side of him, an older, motherly sort, said, "It means to come forth in a flood or gush, dear, or to cast forth in great quantity."

Wilson looked from one crow to another, then back at the door.

"You gotta be kidding," he said. "I have *never* seen a house spew food before. Dudes, houses *don't* spew food!"

"This one does," the first crow said.

"How do you know?" Wilson asked.

"It spews every single morning at the same time," the crow replied. "They say it has for years. We call it Old Faithful."

"Wow!" Wilson said, and whistled under his breath. "Hey, I'm Wilson. I'm new to the neighborhood."

"I'm Carla," said the motherly one.

"Carl," said the other, not taking his eyes off the door.

"Carl, be polite," Carla said. "Didn't I tell you to look someone in the eye when you first meet them? He's my son," she said to Wilson, "bit of a glutton, but generally good natured. He just hatched this spring."

"Hey, me too!" Wilson replied, but soon realized there would be no talking with Carl until after he ate his breakfast.

Someone moved behind a large window and the flock began to murmur. Wilson noticed a least a dozen squirrels lurking in the branches around him, and several others up the hill waiting in the woods.

"Get ready," Carla said, watching the door.

The murmuring grew louder, and Wilson began to feel nervous. He'd never heard of such an event and he didn't know if it was dangerous. He wondered if he'd have to dodge flying chunks of stale bread crust.

"Get set," Carla said, and Wilson heard the back door creak as it swung inwards.

"Go!" Carla cried out and the flock descended as handful after handful of peanuts began to spew from the back door of the little white house.

Squirrels raced down every side of the tree and pandemonium broke out below as they vied for breakfast with crows and a crew of titmice.

Carl, however, stayed in the tree next to Wilson. He was too stunned to move.

"Aren't you gonna go get some?" Wilson asked.

"I'm waiting for the dog food," Carl replied.

"Dog food?" Wilson repeated.

"Yup! About a minute after they toss the peanuts out this door, they throw a bucket of wet dog food out the other door."

"There's another door that spews?" Wilson asked, wondering what kind of house he had come across.

"Dog food's pretty good stuff," Carl said. "Wait – do you hear that?"

A second later Wilson heard another door creak on the other side of the house.

"Let's go," Carl shouted and he took off and swooped over the roof with Wilson right behind him.

They landed on a white picket fence that surrounded a flower filled yard and a little pond. Wilson saw three ducks race towards a mess of wet dog food pellets scattered across the yard. One was a huge black duck with a white belly and a lot of red on his face. The other two were smaller, white ducks. A very young goose took up the rear, and they all attacked the dog food as if they hadn't eaten in days.

"Dude, they're *hungry*," Wilson said, thinking of his own growling stomach.

"Nah," Carl said. "Give 'em a minute and they'll clear out."

Wilson watched them sucking down pellets and thought he might want to head back over to the peanuts and get his share before they were all gone.

"How's it taste?" he asked Carl. "The dog food?"

"Delicious," Carl said. "You can get peanuts anyplace, but dog food is a rare delicacy. Hang on a second."

As he spoke the ducks lost interest and began to wander off. Carl hopped off the fence and grabbed a chunk of food. Wilson followed and nibbled at a bite.

"Not bad!" Wilson said. "A bit strong, but I could get used to it."

He took another bite.

"Mmmm," he said. "Dude, they toss this out every day?"

"Ebery bay," Carl mumbled through a mouthful of food.

"I could get used to this," Wilson said. "What's this place called?"

"Locket's Meadow Farm," Carl said, "but Mom likes to call it

5

'Happily Ever After Farm.' She says once an animal arrives here, they never leave."

"I like it here," Wilson said, wolfing down another chunk of dog food. "I like it a lot."

Chapter Two

Locket and Duck

There are lots of butterflies at Locket's Meadow in August. They flutter from the wildflower gardens at the top of the hill down to the beds of pink and white lilies, over to the butterfly bushes next to the chicken pen and then on to the tufts of tall lavender near the pond by the farm house. There, three ducks and a goose stood preening their feathers following their afternoon bath.

"Hey! Hey you!" called the large, black duck, who was rightfully named Duck, to a bright orange monarch butterfly. "Hey . . . butterfly! If you do me a favor, I'll tell you a secret!"

Most butterflies know better than to trust an oversized duck with a bill as large as a clothespin. This butterfly paused at the very top of a lavender spire and sniffed once in his direction. Then she fluttered high into the air and up the hill towards the pink coneflowers.

"Yeah, hey, thanks a lot! You're a big help!" Duck called after her. "Yeah, whenever you need a favor, I'll be right there for ya!"

Duck hopped onto his favorite tall rock.

"I hate butterflies," he said. "They're all stuck up."

"Not at all," said Buttercup, the larger white duck. "They just can't be bothered with the likes of you."

"They think you'll gobble them right up," said Sunny, the smaller white duck.

"But I don't eat butterflies," Duck said, then shouted up the hill after the butterfly, "I eat *dog food*!"

"You are an odd duck," Sunny muttered, preening an extended wing.

"Duck's a duck?" asked the very young goose.

"Never you mind, Percival," Buttercup said. "There's time enough to figure out what he is later."

Duck was a misunderstood animal, even to himself. Many people who saw him for the first time guessed he was a turkey, and with all his red markings on his face and neck, the confusion was understandable. Duck had a special talent – he could make all the feathers on top of his head stand on end making him look like he had a giant Mohawk hairdo. It made him look more like a rock star than a duck, adding to his identity crisis.

Duck remembered very little of his early life. He knew he'd hatched, he remembered foraging around in an old shed for scraps of moldy bread, and he remembered being snatched up by an indignant teenager in pigtails who fumed about cruelty to animals. She brought him home to Locket's Meadow and raised him in the kitchen in a guinea pig cage, feeding him dog food softened in warm water.

The teenager's name was Bo, and while she called him Duck he didn't much remember what it meant to be a duck since he was so young when he'd moved into the kitchen and spent all his time on the floor with the dogs. From them he learned how to make panting noises and he never did quite learn how to quack. He also learned to wag his tail when he was happy.

At this moment, he wasn't very happy with butterflies in general, and wondered if they tasted anything like dog food.

"You want something done," he said, "you gotta do it yourself."

Duck was no ordinary farm duck. He was of the Muscovy duck family, a large breed with broad wings, capable of flying short distances with either a running start or a tall perch to jump from. To get over the white picket fence he had to climb onto the tallest garden rock and flap his tremendous wings which gave him just enough lift to get over the fence and into the back yard.

9

"Preparing for take off!" he shouted and hopped onto the rock. He began to flap as hard as he could, causing dozens of daisies to lean away and drop their petals. "Lift off!" he cried, and barreled over the fence, landing hard on his chest.

"Oooph! Stupid butterflies," he mumbled and waddled up the hill towards the horse barn.

The barn was just past the chicken pen, and Duck noticed the rooster, Wiggy, was no where in sight so he could tease the chickens without getting pecked. He strutted past the two hens, gloating.

"Wish you could fly, dontcha!" he taunted.

The hens, Harriet and Henrietta, had their wings clipped to keep them from flying out of the pen and going into the woods where the foxes could get them. They both turned their backs on him.

"Who cares?" they clucked in unison.

"Can't a duck get any respect?" he muttered, and walked into the barn.

"Calypso, what's the good word?" Duck said to the old pony. "Any news on the new baby horses today?"

"They're called foals, Duck, and no, there's nothing new," the old pony said, leaning over her stall door. "At least from what I've heard."

"Falstaff," Duck said to the largest horse, a huge brown paint

10

with white spots and a black mane and tail. "Have you been to the big barn today?"

"Yup," Falstaff said, barely glancing up from his pile of hay.

"Anything new?"

"Nope," the huge horse replied. Falstaff was a horse of few words, and if he'd had his own way, his entire day would consist of one big long meal.

"James?"

"Didn't go over today," answered the spotted appaloosa.

"Well, then, I'll just be on my way," Duck said. "No one here knows anything, anyway."

"Duck," Calypso said. "If we knew anything, we'd tell you."

"Promise?" Duck asked.

"Promise," Calypso replied.

Calypso was known to be a very patient and honest horse. She was twenty-seven years old and still working. She did three riding lessons each day, and despite her age she looked very young. Calypso was a lovely dark brown bay pony and her white knee socks on her front legs made her look like a schoolgirl.

While Calypso was a patient soul, Duck was not. He wanted information, and he couldn't wait for it.

"Locket! Hey, Locket!" he waddled towards the opposite end of the barn and called out towards the paddock behind it. "Any news on the babies?"

"Why do I even bother talking to him?" Calypso sighed and drew her head back into her stall.

Yet, she liked Duck very much in spite of himself. His enthusiasm was contagious, even if it was sometimes overwhelming.

Locket stood at the back gate. She and the Arab mare, Classy, were inseparable and shared a large stall and a small pen at the back of the barn.

"What's up, Duck?" she asked, gazing at him through her long, dark eyelashes.

Locket was a beautiful, dark gray burro. She was especially lovely in the warm summer months when her coat was short and sleek. In the winter, her hair grew so long, she nearly doubled in size.

"Any news on the babies?" Duck asked.

"I would only know what the horses tell me," Locket replied, "and they haven't had any news."

"Yes, but *you'd* tell me the truth," Duck said.

"I told you the truth!" Calypso called from inside the barn.

"No, Duck," Locket said. "I know nothing new."

Locket never left the girls' paddock. She had been rescued many years earlier from Death Valley, a huge desert in California. At that time, there were so many wild donkeys and burros running loose in the area that the park rangers decided they were eating too many of the fragile dessert plants and most of the animals would have to be killed. A group of people who loved burros felt sorry for them and offered to capture them and adopt them out to homes around the country.

Locket was one of the lucky ones. She was rescued and brought to Bethany, Connecticut, all the way from the other side of the country. She had decided that was enough distance for a burro to have traveled in her life and was content to stay right there in her paddock with the other ladies. She shared her meadow with Doc and Ezzie, the goats; Cressida and Calypso, the ponies; and Classy, the elegant white Arabian. She had hay, grain, carrots, lots of affection, and best of all, good friends.

While Locket looked like an ordinary burro, there was something unusual about her. Locket could see and hear the farm ghost, Michael. And Michael could see and hear her. They had many conversations, and Locket was the reason Michael didn't cause more mischief around the farm than he already did.

"So, um, Locket," Duck asked. "Maybe you could consult with your, uh, private source? See if he knows anything?"

Locket sighed.

"Duck, I know nothing," Locket said. "Why don't you go to the big barn and ask for yourself?"

"Eh, too far," Duck said. "And I don't trust some of those boarder horses. I hear they tell stories."

Both Locket and Duck knew that was only partly the truth

– Duck never went to the big barn because the winding path through the woods was dangerous for a slow moving bird. There were hawks and foxes and sometimes even coyotes. The boarders were horses whose owners paid rent for them to live in the big barn on the farm and they were a mystery to the animals at the other end of the path.

"Don't believe the rumors about the boarders," Locket said. "I hear they're a nice bunch of horses."

"I don't see you going over there," Duck said.

"Eh, too far," Locket replied, smiling a huge, toothy grin.

Duck knew Locket was just as interested in the newcomers as he was. They had both heard there were two foals arriving soon and they were thought to be very wild.

"They've never been handled by people before," Locket heard Kathleen tell her husband, David. "It's a big project we're getting ourselves into."

David and Kathleen owned the farm, and they, along with their daughter Bo, were always rescuing one animal or another. Somehow they found the time to take care of them and the space to house them, even if it meant having their kitchen table taken up by a cage or two for a few weeks at a time.

Locket was worried about the new foals. She understood what it was like to be frightened and feeling lost and alone in a new place. She remembered her own rescue, and at the time

14

she'd thought it was the end of the world. Hundreds of donkeys were crammed together in a paddock and forced through narrow chutes where they were stabbed with needles so the veterinarians could test their blood for diseases. Then they were forced onto long trailers where they stayed for days and days, barely able to tell day from night. Sometimes, a few animals would be taken off the trailer and those that remained were afraid for them. At least while they were on the trailer, they knew they were all alive.

Locket had never seen people before she was rounded up and sent on her trip to the other side of the country. At the time she hoped when it was all over she would never see any again. She later learned the long ride in the trailer had spared her life. She also learned it was very nice to be brushed and hugged and loved by her new human family.

"If I hear anything new, I'll tell you," Locket said. "And if you hear anything, you tell me."

"It's a deal," Duck said, smiling. They both knew he'd tell the entire farm as soon as he learned any news, whether they wanted to hear it or not. Keeping a secret was not one of Duck's greater talents.

"I have an idea," Duck said. "I'll ask the parrots."

"They won't talk to you," Locket said. "They think they're better than us because they live in the house."

"Hey, I used to live in the house!" Duck said.

15

"Used to," Locket reminded him.

"It's worth a try," he said.

Duck puffed himself up and marched back to the house and around to a window beneath the towering pine tree.

The window was open and Duck could see Polonius, the African Grey parrot, preening on her perch.

"Hey! Hey, bird!" Duck shouted through the window.

"You don't have to shout," Polonius replied. "I can hear you. And I believe you know my name."

"Yeah, yeah," Duck said. "Hey, any news from inside on the new baby horses that are coming?"

"You mean the foals?" Polonius asked from her tall perch. "Why should I tell you?"

"Because if you don't, I'll stand here and talk to you until they lock me in my pen for the night. Then I'll come back in the morning and start all over again."

Polonius shifted from one foot to another, considering Duck's threat.

"Mom!" she called out. "Mom! Close the window!"

"She's not home from work yet," Duck said.

The parrot sighed. Duck was a pest, but she admired his nerve. Most of the outside birds were afraid to speak to the inside parrots because they knew how to talk to people. Who knew what important secrets they'd give away in exchange for an almond or

16

a grape? Duck, having been a house bird for a while, knew more than the other yard birds and had no such fears – he understood the parrots knew the rules of the wild as well as the rules of the kitchen.

"Two weeks, Duck," Polonius said. "I heard them talking over coffee this morning, and they said the foals would be here in two weeks.

"Woohoo! Thanks, bird!" Duck said, and he waddled off to spread the news to everyone, including the snooty butterflies.

Chapter Three

The grass is always greener in someone else's pasture

Cressida, the very fat paint pony with the bright blue eyes, awoke early one morning to find her stall door slightly ajar. She nudged the goats, with whom she shared the stall, and asked, "What do you think?"

Doc and Ezzie uncurled and stretched.

"Don't do it," they heard Calypso say from across the barn aisle. "Just ignore it. David will be out in a minute, and you'll get your breakfast."

But Cressida couldn't ignore it. Neither could the goats. It was one of those late August mornings that smelled faintly of autumn. It was cooler than usual and Cressida thought there might be some new fruit on the ground near the old apple tree. She sniffed the air, trying to catch the scent.

"Cressie, don't do it," Calypso warned again.

Calypso and Cressida had very different ideas about behavior and life in general. The only thing they had in common was they were both ponies. Calypso believed in keeping a positive attitude, while Cressida was the most negative horse in the barn. She never, *ever* smiled. Calypso liked being reliable, hard-working and beloved by children and their parents alike. She had been raised to be a good girl, and believed good conduct was its own reward.

Cressida had no such notions about herself. She liked to get out and run, preferably with no one on her back. If a child had enough nerve to try to ride her she got them out of the saddle and onto the ground as quickly as possible. She lived by the motto, "Life is short, eat as much as you like, escape often and play hard." Once Cressida got loose she stayed loose for as long as she could, or at least until the next meal was about to be served.

Doc stretched from her front feet all the way through to her back feet, then slid up against the stall door as if scratching her side. It slid open a little further.

"Doc!" Calypso warned. "What kind of example are you setting for your daughter?"

19

"I'm just having a scratch," Doc said.

"Momma, can I have a scratch, too?" Ezzie asked.

"Well, if you have an itch, you certainly may," Doc replied.

Ezzie leaned against the door and rubbed her belly along it. It opened a few more inches.

"We're just having a few early morning itches," Cressida said to Calypso. "Nothing more than that."

Calypso gave up and turned her back on them. She had said her piece and her conscience was clear. She wished she had Locket's talents and could converse with that troublesome ghost, Michael, who opened the stall doors if the second latch wasn't properly done. Apparently, he'd paid a visit the night before. She would love to give him a piece of her mind, she would.

Calypso took a bite of leftover hay as she heard a goat take another long rub up against the stall door which squealed as it slid wide open.

Wilson and Carl were sitting in the tall pine tree waiting for Old Faithful to begin spewing food when they noticed a short, fat pony bolt out of the barn and over to the apple tree. She was followed closely by a white goat and a brown goat. The pony began to pick tiny apples off the ground while the goats stood on their hind legs and propped their front feet high against the tree and munched on the lower leaves.

Seconds later, the back door opened and peanuts began to

spew, but only a handful hit the ground before someone in the house shouted, "Pony's out! Goats, too!"

The back door burst open and a man wearing a T-shirt and red boxer shorts sprinted outside. He was followed by a woman wearing sweatpants and an orange plaid flannel shirt. Squirrels and crows scattered up the hill, upset by the disturbance in their morning routine.

"Get a bucket of feed and some carrots," the woman said. "Move slowly!"

"So much for breakfast," muttered Carl.

But Wilson was very interested in what was happening down below. It looked exciting.

"Dude, I think this is gonna be fun!" Wilson said, craning his neck to see through the branches. "Come on!"

He flew to the very top of the tree from where they could see the entire farm, followed closely by Carl.

The goats munched leaves as the pony nibbled grass, warily watching the couple as they slipped into the barn. They heard the sound of grain poring into a bucket.

"What do you think they'll do?" Wilson asked.

"I say they go for the food," Carl replied.

"If I were them, I'd bolt," said Wilson. "It's a lot more fun. They'll get fed when they get caught later."

The couple walked slowly out of the barn. One of them carried

21

a bucket and the other held a handful of carrots and a rope. The pony eyed the bucket then took a nibble at a fallen apple. She was playing it cool.

The man shook the feed bucket and the goats wavered. The crows could see them struggling with the age-old question; do we want apple leaves or do we want grain?

"Grain," the white goat muttered to the brown goat, and the two of them raced to the man, who led them back into the barn.

"I just lost all my respect for goats, dude!" Wilson muttered.

"Shhh! Watch that pony," Carl said.

The pony picked up another small apple and munched it, warily watching the barn door out of the corner of her eye.

"She's gonna bolt," Wilson said.

"Wow! I think you're right," Carl said, getting drawn into the events despite his growling stomach.

The man returned with the bucket of grain and he and the woman slowly approached the pony who carefully picked up one more tiny apple, cautiously chewing it. They were almost right next to her, and the pony leaned in towards the bucket.

"She toying with them, I can tell," Wilson said. "Watch her now!"

The man reached over the pony's neck with the rope and the little horse pretended she was about to eat from the bucket, but instead of eating she bolted right between the two, straight through

22

the barn and out the other side. The couple ran after her.

The pine tree erupted in cheers – the entire flock had been watching the action.

"Let's go!" Carl shouted and the two young crows flew across the yard to the top of the tallest black walnut tree next to the girl's paddock where the view was even better.

Cressida loved to run. For a very fat pony, she could move very, very fast. She raced down the path through the woods and past the indoor riding arena. Just for fun, she cut through the big barn, kicking up her heels at the boarder horses who barely had time to look over their stall doors before Cressida was out the other side and racing up the hill towards the log cabin. She was aiming for one of the top pastures which had a nice supply of rich, green grass, something she enjoyed even more than grain. If she got there quickly enough, she'd have a few minutes of grazing before David and Kathleen arrived with the bucket and rope.

Locket and Classy watched from the pen outside their large stall.

"If she'd let the kids ride her, she'd get to run all the time," Classy said.

Classy loved to go for rides. When Kathleen came to get her each day she trotted right up to her and slid her head into the halter.

"It won't ever happen," Locket said. "She likes the chase even

23

more than she likes the running."

Cressida made it to the top pasture and nosed open the unlocked gate. She grazed as quickly as she could while David and Kathleen walked up the hill towards her.

"No!" Carl shouted from the top of the black walnut tree. "Get out of that field! They'll shut you in! You're caught for sure!"

"Dumb pony!" Wilson mumbled. "She should have kept going."

Falstaff could just see the action from over his stall door.

"That's enough, pony!" he shouted as loudly as he could. "We don't get breakfast until you come back!"

Cressida didn't care. She kept ripping up huge bites of grass. It wasn't every day she had such a lovely opportunity.

When the couple finally reached the field and closed the gate Cressida took off at a gallop and circled the field twice before she stopped and allowed them to drop a rope over her neck. She was a fast pony, but she was also out of shape, out of breath and ready for her second course of breakfast – grain.

Locket watched David lead the pony down the hill until she couldn't see them anymore behind the indoor arena.

"Classy," she whispered. "I heard that voice again last night."

Classy bent her elegant neck close to Locket's head.

"Did it say the same thing?"

"Yes," Locket said, tears coming to her huge, dark eyes. "I don't know what to do. That's two nights in a row."

Classy touched her nose to Locket's.

"It'll be OK," she said.

"Will it?" Locket asked.

The voice she had heard over the past two nights was not at all like the voice of Michael, the farm ghost. It was a very young voice, lost and lonely and small, and it kept saying, over and over, "I want my mommy."

Chapter Four

When you wish upon the moon

Classy had come to Locket's Meadow in the usual way, which meant there was nothing ordinary about her journey to the farm. She had lived on another farm in Connecticut for fifteen years, almost her entire life, and most of the time, she had loved it there. Her owner, however, injured her knees and couldn't ride anymore. For two years, Classy waited patiently in her field and wished for the long, lovely rides through the woods to begin again.

The longer she waited, the more she realized those days were over and she began to dream. While she slept in her pasture under the stars, she dreamed of another farm where there were lots of animals in the field with her. Sometimes it seemed so real she'd wake up and look around, wondering where her friends were. Yet, in the soft moonlight, she always found herself alone.

Other times she dreamed she was trotting down a country lane ridden by a woman with long legs and gentle hands. Together they explored quiet woods and sometimes raced down long stretches of soft, dirt paths. Then, they'd return to a lovely white barn where the woman would rinse Classy off with warm water, towel her dry, comb out her long, white mane and tail and feed her carrots, all the while telling her what a good horse she was.

They were lovely dreams, and Classy would awaken feeling sad these adventures only happened in her sleep. One day, however, she was startled awake from one of her dreams by a voice that said, "Well, where *are* you?"

It was so loud and clear, Classy woke up and scrambled to her feet. It was still dark, and the moon was just a tiny white sliver although the sky was beginning to brighten in the east. The voice echoed in her head.

Classy tilted her head back and whinnied at the slip of moon.

"I'm right here!" she cried into the early morning. "I'm right here!"

She wasn't sure if a wish on a little slip of a moon worked as well as a wish on a full moon, but it was the only moon she had to work with that night so she wished as hard as she could and with all her aching heart.

At Locket's Meadow, Kathleen couldn't sleep. She had been dreaming every night about riding a snow white horse with a trot so smooth and even she felt as if she were flying. It was like riding the mythical unicorn or the winged horse Pegasus, and when she woke in the early morning from her nighttime gallops she felt as light as air.

That particular morning, when she awoke from her dream, she couldn't fall back to sleep. She smelled the fresh, early morning air drifting through the window and she slipped out of bed, pulled on a flannel shirt and stepped outside to look at the sliver of silver moon. For a moment, she thought she saw a winged white horse soar across the sky.

"Well, where *are* you!" she called out to the moon.

When she went back inside, Kathleen turned on the computer,

entered the name of the local horse magazine, and typed into the search box, "Snow white horse for sale."

"Snow white mare," read the ad at the top of the list. "Smooth gaits, some professional training. 15 years old."

"David," she said over coffee that morning. "There's a horse I want to go look at."

"No more horses," David replied. "We have too many as it is."

"But I think this is a special one," she said.

"Kathleen, they are all special ones," David replied. "Let someone else have this special horse for a change."

She took a sip of coffee. "I can't. Are you going to come see her with me or not?"

David sighed. He knew the only way he could possibly talk his wife out of getting another horse was if he was there to stop her from writing a check to the person selling it. The next day he drove with her to the tiny town of Scotland, Connecticut, more than an hour away.

From her field, Classy saw the tall woman with the long blonde pony tail get out of her car. She thought she was still dreaming.

"Is it really her?" she thought, and at that moment she saw the woman spot her, and could feel her thinking the exact same thing.

Classy and Kathleen only half listened to the horse's owner

29

talking about all the wonderful things Classy could do when she used to ride her. The two of them were anxious to get a saddle on Classy's back. Then they would know if each was the one the other had dreamed about.

The owner tacked Classy up and led her to a fenced dirt ring.

"She doesn't like the mounting block," her owner said. "I always just put my foot in the stirrup and swung my leg over."

If she wants to use a mounting block, Classy thought, I could get used to it.

Kathleen swung her leg over the white mare's back, and they began to trot immediately. Once around, twice around, three times around – Classy was beginning to remember how to move under a saddle.

"Come on, pretty girl," Kathleen said. "Put your head down. Let's see what you can do."

Classy curved her graceful Arabian neck in a deep arch and picked her feet up in a high prance. After two more times around Kathleen stopped, patted her on the neck, and got off.

"That's it?" Classy thought. "We were having so much fun!"

They left the horse standing in the paddock.

"We can't," David said, softly so no one else could hear. "We don't have the room."

"We can add on another stall," Kathleen said.

"I'll tell you what," he said. "Bring Cathy up and ask her what she thinks of the mare."

Cathy was their barn manager. She took good care of the boarder horses, and she knew horses better than just about anyone.

"If she likes her, we can think about it," he said, hoping that Cathy would see things his way.

That evening, Kathleen stood in the big barn telling Cathy about the horse she'd seen that day.

"What are you, crazy?" Cathy said. "She hasn't been ridden in years. We have no idea if she's worth anything at all. You could bring her home and find out all she's good for is taking up room in a pasture."

"I don't think so," Kathleen said. "Just come see her. And we'll bring the trailer, just in case."

The next day, a few hours after they had driven away with an empty trailer, Cathy and Kathleen returned to Locket's Meadow. From her paddock, Locket watched as Cathy opened the back gate and let out a beautiful white horse. Kathleen took the lead rope and led the horse down the path through the trees towards the girl's paddock.

They stopped in the barn first and Kathleen fed Classy a carrot before kissing her on the nose and turning her loose in the paddock.

Classy stood just inside the gate, nervous and searching for a

31

friend.

Locket walked directly up to her and said, "Welcome!"

"Am I home?" Classy asked.

"Yes," Locket replied. "Everyone is home here."

Chapter Five

Making room for more

The end of August always brought big changes to Locket's Meadow. The sound of baby birds was replaced by the buzzing and chirping of cicadas, crickets and flies, and the scent of peonies gave way to that of late-blooming roses and freshly delivered hay.

It was a lovely time for everyone, except the horses. The biting flies knew their days were numbered and latched onto as many animals as possible before the first frost came and ended their feeding frenzy.

The horses stood in their fields, stamping their feet and swishing their tails, sides pressed together despite the heat in an effort to avoid being bitten as much as possible.

Duck strutted past Calypso in the girls' paddock and she nudged him with her nose.

"Duck," she said, "aren't you supposed to eat bugs? I have a few here you can help yourself to."

"I don't eat bugs," Duck replied. "I eat dog food."

"What good are you, then," snapped Doc, who felt goats suffered more from the flies than horses did because they had no long tails for swishing them away.

"No good at all," Duck laughed, wagging his tail. "I never said I was useful – just handsome!"

And Duck raised the feathers on the top of his head so they stood straight in the air, forming a perfect Mohawk.

Calypso stamped her foot, perhaps a little closer to Duck than she normally would, and he hopped backwards.

"Ah, what a life you lead," she said. "No work, all play, and handsome to boot!"

Robbie, one of the barn helpers, arrived to bring Calypso next door for afternoon lessons at riding camp.

"Good," she said as he slipped her halter over her nose. "He'll spray me with some more fly spray."

"Pay attention while you're over there," Duck said. "Maybe they'll talk about the new baby horses."

"Yes, yes, more work for the old pony," Calypso said. "I'll see what I can find out, Duck."

It was the last week of summer riding camp, and Calypso was looking forward to the children going back to school so she could have her mornings to herself again. She liked giving lessons, but lately there were so many every day and the weather was still so hot.

Robbie led her down the path and over to the big barn where he tied her in the aisle to saddle her. Cathy, the barn manager, was talking to a group of children outside the tack room door. She held up two photos for the camp kids to look at.

"Does anyone know what a PMU foal is?" she asked them.

Calypso squinted her blue eyes until she could see the photos. One was a paint and the other an appaloosa.

"Are they spotted horses?" one child asked.

"No, not always, but these two are," Cathy replied. "In just a few days these two foals will arrive at Locket's Meadow. If they didn't come here, they would have gone to slaughter and become horse meat. Does anyone know why?"

Calypso shuddered. She didn't want to know the details, but she was tied in the aisle and couldn't get away.

None of the children answered.

"There is a drug called Premarin that's made from the urine of pregnant mares," Cathy said. "Lot's of women take this drug because as they get older, their bodies stop making the hormone

35

estrogen, and their doctors give them Premarin to take as an estrogen replacement. To make it, thousands of mares are kept pregnant all the time, and farmers collect their urine, which has a lot of estrogen in it, and sell it to a company that uses it to make this drug. Because of this, almost 40,000 foals are born every year. These foals are born because their mothers must be pregnant to provide Pregnant Mare Urine, so they're called PMU foals. What do you think happens to these babies?"

"They come here?" asked one child.

"We can only bring a few of them here," Cathy said. "There aren't enough homes and farms for these babies to go to, and the farmers don't have room to keep them all, so they have to get rid of them somehow. There are lots of countries where they eat horsemeat, so they're sent to feedlots to get fattened up before they're shipped off to the slaughter houses. Almost half of them are killed."

The children stood silently. Calypso could hardly breathe and she no longer noticed the flies gnawing on her legs. Is that why there was so much whispering about the new foals coming in? As long as she'd been alive, she'd never seen a farm as abuzz with anticipation as Locket's Meadow was over these foals and this farm had seen a lot of rescued animals come down its long driveway.

"I want to bring one home," said Lucy, who was one of

Calypso's favorite little girls. "I'll ask my daddy."

"It's not easy," Cathy said. "They're very wild. The babies are born out in huge pastures, mostly up in Canada, and when they're only about four months old, they're separated from their mothers, who have to go back into their stalls in the barns so the farmers can start collecting their urine again. The babies have hardly seen any people, and they're very frightened. They don't know why they've been taken away from their mothers or why they're put in trailers and taken far away from their mothers."

"When did all this start?" asked another little girl named Brittany. "I've never heard of it before."

"It's been happening for a long time," Cathy said, "about 50 years."

"That's sick!" Brittany said. "Why would anyone eat a horse?"

"Why would anyone want to take a drug made out of horse pee?" asked Ethan. "I'm glad men don't have to take it."

"I can't believe how mean the farmers are," said Lucy.

"The farmers are trying to make a living and feed their families," Cathy said. "Just like farmers who raise pigs and cows and chickens for food. As long as women take Premarin, PMU farmers will keep mares pregnant and collect urine. And as long as we have a farm, we'll keep PMU foals here. You guys are lucky – you'll get to learn what it's like to raise a foal."

Calypso had thought she'd heard everything, but this was all new to her. She wanted to get right back to the other barn to tell Locket what she had learned.

"Ethan, where's your riding helmet?" Cathy asked. "You aren't getting on a horse without one. And Robbie, why isn't Calypso tacked and ready to go? Robbie? OK, where's Robbie, now? All right, someone else tack Calypso."

Brittany slid a saddle pad over Calypso's back while the old pony wondered how she was going to get through her lessons that afternoon. She simply wasn't feeling very well.

Back at the little white farm house, Kathleen was also struggling with how she would get through work that day. She couldn't decide if all the buzzing she heard was from the bugs humming outside her window or if her brain was just working way too hard.

Kathleen sat at her computer trying to decide what she was going to write about for her weekly newspaper column, but she couldn't focus. Mostly, she was trying to think of a way to explain to David why she had agreed to let a third PMU foal come to Locket's Meadow that fall. She had no idea how to break the news to him this time – the first two foals had been hard enough to explain.

She stared out the window at the dozens of yellow butterflies dancing above the wildflower beds and thought about all the other times she'd brought home rescued animals and how David eventually grew to love every one of them.

She turned back to the computer screen. This time, she decided David would learn about their newest horse in the newspaper. She didn't feel like explaining it in person. He always got the newspaper at his office first thing in the morning and turned to his wife's column to see what she had to say about him that week. Perhaps by the time he got home that evening, he'd have grown used to the idea. At least, she hoped he would. She knew she sometimes asked a little too much of her poor husband.

Chapter Six

The truth about the rest of the world

The hundreds of daisies in the wildflower meadow followed the sun as it crossed the sky each day. By late afternoon their smiling faces all turned uphill towards the back pasture where the big geldings, Falstaff and James, stood waiting to be brought in for supper. At this time of day the girls usually waited at the gate near the barn, but today they stood crowded at the back of their paddock near the boys while they all listened to Calypso tell her story.

"I've never heard of such a thing, Calypso," Falstaff said. "That's disgusting!"

"But it's what she said," Calypso insisted. "There are people who eat baby horses!"

"Momma, do people eat baby goats?" Ezzie asked Doc.

"Certainly not!" Doc replied, "And I don't think you should be scaring my kid, old pony!"

Wiggy, the ancient rooster, was standing on Locket's back. He'd listened to Calypso's story, and was the only one not surprised.

"Most places are not like Locket's Meadow," Wiggy said. "I've heard stories that would chill you to the bone. Once, years ago, I knew a hen named Bernice who had lived in a terrible place. She was trapped in a tiny cage all day surrounded by thousands of other chickens in tiny cages which made it easier for the farmer to collect their eggs. One day, when the farmer decided the hens weren't laying enough eggs, he packed them into crates and stacked them on the back of a truck and sent them to be killed."

The other animals gasped.

"Impossible!" said James. "Why would they do that?"

"To make soup, is what Bernice had heard," Wiggy replied.

"Soup?" Classy said. "I can't believe it!"

"How did she escape?" Cressida asked, always looking for inspiration.

"The crate she was in fell off the back of the truck," Wiggy said, "and someone found her near the road and brought her to Kathleen because they knew she had other chickens. Bernice was so frightened, she could barely cluck. She settled in fine, though – she even started laying eggs again. Big redhead, she was, very attractive."

Wiggy hopped from the middle of Locket's back right up to the top of her head and peered out from between her huge, fuzzy ears.

"I don't mean to scare you," he said. "But most of the world is not like here. We're safe, we're the lucky ones."

Duck poked his head between the fence rails and looked up at Calypso.

"I talked to one of the house birds today," he said. "She heard the babies are on their way, but they're coming from so far away it'll take a long time – maybe days."

"Days and days," Locket said, remembering the long trip she once took to get to her new meadow.

Just then, two young crows swooped out of the sky and landed on Locket's back.

"Do I *look* like a bus?" she asked and shook so hard all three birds went flying.

"Sorry," Wilson said from the fence rail where he'd landed. "The rooster looked like he was having a good time, so we thought we'd hop on and catch a ride, too."

"Where is your mother?" Locket asked Carl, who was now perched on the edge of a water tank. "She really should be keeping an eye on you!"

"I dunno," he replied. "She said she'd be back in an hour and we should keep each other out of trouble until she returned."

"Children keeping children out of trouble – I've never seen *that* work before," Calypso said. "Wait until I see that Carla!"

"Calypso," Locket said. "I'm going to go wait for dinner at the barn gate. Would you keep me company?"

She winked at Classy, who joined the two ladies as they walked across the paddock and huddled in the corner, their three faces nearly touching.

"I think I know where that voice is coming from," Locket said.

"What voice?" Calypso asked.

"For the past two nights, I've heard a voice," Locket said, "and it wasn't Michael's."

"Who was it, then?" Calypso asked.

"I can't be sure," she replied, "but it keeps saying, 'I want my mommy.'"

"One of the foals?" Calypso gasped.

"Maybe," Classy said. "Have you tried to talk to it?"

"No," Locket said. "I mean, how can I?"

43

"You talk to Michael," Classy said.

"Yes, but he's right there," Locket said. "I can see him. How can you talk to someone you can't see?"

"It's not so hard," Classy answered. "If you want it badly enough, if you feel it with your heart, you can reach out to anyone. I didn't even know I was doing it, but Kathleen and I somehow understood each other long before we even knew each other existed. We still do," Classy said. "We always know what each other is feeling."

"But how?" Locket asked. "*How* do you do it?"

Classy thought about it. How *did* they find each other? She really wasn't sure, except she knew they simply were meant to be together. It didn't make any sense, and yet Classy knew that making sense was not as important as it seemed.

"I can't tell you exactly how to do it," Classy said. "But it isn't like talking with your mouth or with your head. It's like talking with your heart. It sounds really hard to do, but once you understand it, it's the easiest kind of talking there is."

Cressida had quietly walked up behind the other ladies and now poked her head into the corner alongside them.

"Hearing voices again, Locket?" she asked. "Maybe it's another ghost."

"No, no," Locket replied. "I can't see this one. I think it might be one of the babies who are on their way here."

44

"Oh, the poor thing, if it is!" Calypso said. "It must be so scared! I hope it didn't hear any of that talk about feed lots and slaughter houses."

"Hello, ladies!" Kathleen said, poking her head out the barn door. "What are you all chatting about?" she asked when she saw their four faces pressed close together. "Dinner will be ready in just a minute! And later, Miss Classy, we're going for a nice, long ride."

While Classy knew Kathleen had said they were going for a ride, what she *felt* her say was very different. In her heart, Classy knew she really meant, "I'm in really big trouble now, horse, and the only thing that will make me feel better is some time with you."

"Hey! Hey ladies!" Duck poked his head through the barn door. "I just talked to the house bird, and she said David and Kathleen were just arguing. And guess what about?"

"What, Duck?" Locket asked.

"We now have *three* foals coming to Locket's Meadow!"

Chapter Seven

Just one more baby

There was a lot of worrying at Locket's Meadow that night. Kathleen sat in her darkened office with Polonius perched on her shoulder. She was staring at a computer screen filled with pictures of foals that would go to slaughter if no one adopted them. The photos had been posted by a group that had convinced some Canadian PMU farmers to give them a chance to find homes for some of their foals before they sent them to the feedlots. The foal adopters would pay the farmers the same price as what the feedlots were paying, and the foals would then be shipped to new homes all over the United States and Canada.

Kathleen had agreed to take in a foster foal, which was one of the leftovers that no one had yet adopted. They would keep it at Locket's Meadow and try to find a new home for it. David was very upset. He said they didn't have room for another foal and babies required a lot time and work. With both David and Kathleen working their regular jobs, and Bo away at college for most of the year, the next few months promised to be a lot of hard work trying to take care of everything.

Also, there was another problem they ran into every time they brought a new animal to the farm. In spite of their best intentions, which were to rescue animals until another good home could be found, no animals ever left Locket's Meadow – once they arrived, they always stayed. Kathleen had promised David this foal would be placed in a new home within the first month, but he didn't believe her.

And yet, how could she not let it come to their farm? There were only a few days left before this batch of foals would be sent to the feed lots. And to add to the problem, Kathleen had learned two other farmers had decided to let the adoption group post photos of their foals on the website and there were only a few weeks to get the new ones adopted before they, too, would go to the feedlots to be fattened up for slaughter. Winter came early in Canada and it was too expensive for the farmers to keep their extra foals and feed them through the cold months.

Kathleen thought about it late into the night. She knew she couldn't adopt 20,000 foals and put all of them on their little ten acre farm. But she was a writer and a newspaper reporter. Maybe she could figure out another way to help save them. She decided to write a letter to the women at the website and offer them her help.

While Kathleen wrote her letter, David sat at the kitchen table with three of their five house cats lounging on the floor near his feet. He added up how much it cost to feed and take care of every horse and animal at Locket's Meadow. He added in how much it would cost to put up new fencing and sheds and stalls. He wrote down all the really important reasons why they couldn't take in any more horses and why the foster foal would have to move on to another home as quickly as possible. He had lots and lots of reasons.

That morning, after his newspaper had arrived, he'd gotten himself a cup of coffee and settled in at his desk to read his wife's articles and column. Kathleen wrote one column a week on any topic she wanted, and often he was the topic. This week, she had written about the foals that would arrive in a few days, about the many of them that still hadn't been adopted, and how some would be fostered. She also wrote that a foster foal would be coming to Locket's Meadow.

David nearly dropped his newspaper when he read this, but

somehow managed to read the last paragraph, which said, "My husband, Poor David, doesn't know about the third foal, yet, but as soon as he reads this column, he will! If he's not in the best mood today, I apologize – it's my fault. Those who work in his office, feel free to give me a call and warn me if I'll be coming home to a husband in a 'foal mood' tonight!"

David didn't wait until he got home. He picked up the phone and called his wife immediately.

"Are you kidding?" he said when Kathleen answered the phone. "You *know* what will happen if that horse comes to this farm."

"No, I promise we'll find it a new home," she said.

"You can't! You never can!" he replied. "How many cats have you brought in and promised you'd find another home for?"

"This is different," she said.

"Yes," he replied. "It's bigger and more expensive and more work and when you fall in love and can't part with it, it's a much bigger problem."

"I don't have to keep every horse that comes here," she said.

"Prove it!" he said and slammed the phone down.

He sat at his desk fuming for a few minutes before picking the phone up again and called the Dick Farrell Feed and Supply Shop to find out how much a new paddock would cost.

When David got home that night he walked straight to the

barn. James and Falstaff poked their heads out of their stalls and nickered a greeting and he stopped to rub their faces. He loved the horses, he really did. He just needed to know there wouldn't be any more – enough was enough. At least one person in the family had to be practical. And while Kathleen seemed to think it was her job to rescue every endangered animal on the planet, David knew it was impossible.

That night, while the house sat dark and quiet, each person brooding in their own room, Locket stood outside under the stars, waiting. She was beginning to wonder if she had imagined the voice. What if she didn't hear it again? Worse than that, what if she *did* hear it and couldn't find a way to make it hear her? The responsibility was almost more than she could bear. She wished Classy could hear this voice since she was the one who knew how to do all this "talking from the heart."

The frogs in the duck pond were tuning up for their evening performance. Some worked on their baritone harrumphs while others perfected their alto ribbits. The crickets in the wildflower gardens were in full concert and an occasional coyote let loose with a howl. Locket was lulled by the familiar sounds and she slowly relaxed and thought about singing along with the other night creatures. She began to hum, looking for a harmony. She had almost forgotten about the babies when once again she heard the sad, small voice say, "I want my mommy."

Locket gasped.

"I want my mommy," it said again.

The burro was not sure how to react. How could she talk to someone who wasn't even there? Even though Michael was a ghost, she could see exactly where he was when he was in the barn. Where was this little voice coming from, she thought?

"I'm where it's dark," she heard it say. "I'm where there are no mommies."

Locket nearly sank to her knees. Whoever it was could read her thoughts! She had to decide what she should think next.

"Are you alone?" she asked.

"No, there are lots of us in here," it said, "but there are fewer now. Sometimes, some of us leave."

"And go where?" Locket asked, amazed at how easy this kind of talking was.

"We don't know," the voice said. "They don't come back. Do you know where we're going?"

"I know where you are," Locket thought. "I've been there. It's very scary."

"What's going to happen?" it asked.

"I'm not sure," Locket replied. "I don't know . . . maybe . . . I just don't know for sure."

"Does my mommy know where I am?"

"Maybe," Locket thought. "Maybe she does.

51

"Who are you?" it asked.

"I'm Locket," she answered. "I live on a lovely little farm, and I'm hoping you are coming here."

"Is there a mommy there?"

"Yes," Locket said. "There's a very nice mommy here."

Chapter Eight

The jailbirds squawk

Every morning, David woke up long before the sun rose and followed the exact same routine. He made a pot of coffee and poured himself a cup which he drank while he wrote a list of things he had to do that day. Then he poured himself a second cup and carried it outside with him to the do the morning feeding and chores.

As soon as the ducks heard the creak of the backdoor they clamored for David to let them out of their pens and into the yard. He turned them loose and they raced to the pond for their first swim of the morning. Then he opened the gate and walked up the hill, always pausing to take a big, deep breath of clean, early morning air.

Next he let the chickens loose from their cage and they jumped out and began to scratch the soil in their yard, hoping to find some early worms and bugs.

David then went into the barn to measure horse feed into buckets. Falstaff stomped his foot impatiently and James kicked the wall of his stall. Locket sang her early morning food song which sounded a lot like a motorcycle revving its engine.

David didn't know a lot about riding or raising horses, but he was very good at taking care of them. He loved doing the early morning chores in the barn. The grain smelled sweet and fresh and the splashes of water from the water bucket felt good and clean against his arms. The horses were always bleary-eyed and their manes and tails had bits of hay and wood shavings clinging to them from sleeping on the floor. As tired as they were, they were always happy to see him and even happier when he gave them their grain.

When they were done eating David turned them all out in

their fields. The boys went to the big back pasture and the girls stayed in their paddock behind the barn. The boys usually stood nose to nose and munched their hay while the girls lined up along the fence and ate theirs. Today, however, they all ignored the hay and crowded near each other along the gate between their fields. Seconds later, the old rooster flew out of his pen and raced up the hill to join them. Right behind him ran Duck who had skipped his bath in favor of flying over the fence and heading up the hill.

It seemed odd to David, but he didn't have time to investigate. He had to shower, eat breakfast and get to the office.

"So, did you hear it again?" Cressida asked Locket.

"Yes," Locket replied.

"What did it say?" Doc asked.

"It still wants its mommy," she said. "And it said there are lots of others with it, and it's dark where they are. It sounds like they're in a trailer."

"What else?" Classy asked.

"Nothing," Locket said. "It just said that someone was opening the door and then it didn't say anything else. Next thing I knew, Michael showed up looking to cause trouble and I spent the rest of the night trying to talk him out of going into the house and turning on the radios."

"Did it work?" Doc asked.

"I think so" Locket replied.

"Those poor babies," Doc said. "They must be so frightened."

"Yes," Locket said. "I know they are."

Kathleen was sitting at the kitchen table drinking coffee and writing her own list of things she had to do that day when David came inside from doing chores. She was feeling a little lonely because Bo had left to go back to college in Boston and wouldn't be home again for a long time. Also, she knew David was still angry with her about the extra foal. Polonius sat on her shoulder holding the cap to Kathleen's pen in her beak and making kissing noises in her ear to cheer her up.

"I have to go to the office early today," she said. "I have a phone interview at 9 a.m., then I have to write for most of the day. I'll be home in time for afternoon chores."

"I have to . . ." David said, then paused. He could tell she was still upset with him. "I have to . . . oh, I don't want to be fighting with you, Kathleen. We'll just deal with whatever happens with the horses. It'll be fine."

"We don't have to keep them all, David," she said. "We'll find a home for the foster foal."

"OK," he replied. "OK. We'll do whatever we have to do. I just don't want to fight."

"Neither do I," Kathleen said.

She stood and hugged him, forgetting Polonius was on her

shoulder.

"Hey!" Polonius said, dropping the pen cap. "Hey, look out!"

"Sorry," Katheen said.

The phone rang.

"Answer it!" Polonius said. "Hellooooo!"

"It's pretty early for someone to call," David said. "It must be your sister."

Kathleen went into the bedroom to answer it and came out a minute later.

"It's the hauler," she said. "He said they drove through the night and now he's taking a short break. They expect to be here tonight!"

"With the babies?"

"With the babies!"

Kathleen could hardly breathe, she was so excited.

"Finally! They're finally coming!" she screamed.

"Put me *down*!" Polonius screeched.

The bird could barely hang onto Kathleen's shoulder as she jumped up and down with excitement, so Kathleen put Polonius back in her cage.

Outside in the pine tree a large group of crows and squirrels wondered why breakfast was so late spewing from the house. They were accustomed to being fed on time at Locket's Meadow. Wilson and Carl flew to a low branch and peered into the kitchen window.

"They're just standing in there talking," Wilson said. "What could be more important than spewing? Geez!"

"Hey, crow!" said a voice in the next window. "Crow, come here."

Wilson peered inside and saw a bird in a cage looking out the window at him.

"Hey! Dude! What did you do?"

"I beg your pardon?" Polonius said.

"Dude! Why'd they lock you up? You need to get sprung! We can organize a rescue!"

"I certainly do not need to *get sprung*," Polonuis said. "I need you to relay a message for me."

Wilson and Carl flew to the very tip of the branch closest to the window and it bobbed low beneath their weight. Wilson saw several more cages, each one holding large, brightly-colored birds.

"Dude! There's more of you in there! Oh, man, it's like, you're all jailbirds!"

"First of all, my name is not 'Dude,'" Polonius said. "Second, we are not here against our will. We have a very nice life inside. Third, I need you to do me a favor."

"You want a metal file baked inside a cake?" Carl snickered.

"Pardon me?" Polonius said.

"You know," Carl snickered again, "a file, to cut the bars of your cage with. So you can escape."

"All right, listen to me carefully," Polonius said. "Tell the duck that the foals are arriving tonight. He'll know what to do."

"What's arriving tonight?" Wilson asked.

"The foals! The foals!" Polonius said. "Oh, forgive me, you don't understand proper English," she sighed, then said very slowly, "The baby horses will be here this evening. Do you understand? *Tell the duck!*"

"Cool, dude! I get it!" Wilson said. "Hey, can you get this house to spew a little breakfast?"

"As soon as I see the duck go over the fence and head for the barn, I'll make sure they start throwing food," Polonius said.

Wilson and Carl took off, and less than a minute later, Polonius watched Duck fly over the fence and waddle up the hill towards the barn.

The crows made it back to the tree just as the peanuts began to spew from the house.

"Wow," Carl said. "We made a good connection – that jail bird delivers!"

Chapter Nine

The messenger duck

"Bird!" Duck called inside the house to Polonius. "Hey, bird!"

"What now, Duck?" Polonius said from her cage. "Make it fast – we're watching a TV show about dogs. They say they're intelligent – imagine that!"

The house birds held a low opinion of dogs.

"I got the message and passed it on," Duck said. "Did they say what time they're coming?"

"No, they just said it would be late tonight," Polonius answered.

"The horses want to know what stalls the babies are going

into," Duck said.

"They aren't coming to this barn," Polonius replied. "They're going to stay at the big boarder barn for now."

"WHAT?" Duck shouted. "They aren't gonna be boarders, are they? We thought they were staying!"

"They are, Duck! Calm down!" Polonius said. "Listen carefully, because I'm only going to say this once and then I'm going back to my TV program. The foals have to be quarantined for thirty days, which means they can't be near any other horses."

"Why? What did they do wrong? And what's carrotined?" He had a vision of foals being pelted with carrots.

"Nothing!" Polonius said. "They have to be kept away from all the other horses just in case they're sick. They're coming from far away and we have to make sure they're healthy."

Duck did not want to be the one to tell this to the horses. If the boarders met the babies before horses on this side of the path did, they weren't going to be very happy about it.

"You said thirty days, bird?"

"Yes, thirty days, Duck," Polonius replied. "Now, if you'll excuse me, the commercials are over. We're going to watch how they train dogs to play fetch. Imagine – chasing a ball and bringing it back, just because some human tells you to. Ridiculous!"

Polonius turned her back on the window, and Duck slowly wandered up the hill to the barn. He didn't much care for the message he was carrying today.

Every evening as the sun set, Kathleen and David took a stroll around the farm. First they checked on the gardens and the pond. Then, they herded the ducks, chickens and the baby goose into their pens where they locked them up for the night so they would be safe from coyotes, foxes and raccoons.

The last place they visited was the barn. When Locket saw them coming she began to sing her "carrot" song. Every night before the barn lights were turned off each animal was given a carrot and a goodnight kiss on the nose. It made the animals feel safe and well-loved.

Tonight, they each got extra carrots and kisses before Kathleen and David turned the lights off and walked to the bench next to the duck pond.

"We have some very nice horses," Kathleen said.

"Yes, we do," David replied.

"I think the new ones will be just as wonderful," she said.

The sun was nearly set and bats zigzagged across the deep blue sky, catching mosquitoes and flies in the dim light.

"Want to go to the big barn and wait for them?" David asked.

"Sure," Kathleen replied, and they walked through the woods, hand in hand, anxiously awaiting the arrival of their new babies.

"There they go," Cressida said as the couple walked past the barn door. "The babies must be arriving soon."

"I can't believe they're staying with the boarders!" Calypso said. "They should be over here where they're going to live for the rest of their lives! Who is going to take care of them? We barely *know* any of those other horses!"

"But Duck said they won't be near the boarders, either," Classy said. "What did he call it? Carrotined?"

"Sounds tasty," Cressida said.

"Sounds lonely," Classy said.

The sky blackened. There was no moon tonight, and the stars burned brighter because of it. The barn was silent aside from an occasional scurrying mouse and Locket paced back and forth outside her stall door hoping to hear the tiny voice again. She thought if she could tell it she was going to be just a short distance from where they were, it would help the foals feel less frightened and alone.

She paced back and forth, then in and out of her stall where Classy was poking through the hay looking for some of the better pieces. Locket stopped to take a bite of hay then left the stall, munching, and came face to face with Michael.

Michael was a small ghost who had at one time been a small man. While he wasn't at all frightening, Locket always tried to make him feel he was doing a good job of haunting the farm.

"Oh!" Locket said. "You scared me!"

"Did I?" Michael said. "Excellent! A perfect way to start the

63

evening!"

"Yes," Locket said. "Now if you would kindly leave it at that, we'll all have a nice night!"

"Hardly the plan I've been working on," Michael said. "I thought I'd start at the big barn and turn on a few lights, then maybe head into the house and change the channel on the TV, then . . ."

"Michael, why don't you just take a nice walk? It's a lovely night," Locket said.

She didn't want him to cause any trouble with the babies arriving so soon.

"Oh, Locket, darling, if you only knew how boring it was to be me and stuck here on this little farm with nothing to do but stir up trouble," Michael said. "I think what they really need in the big barn is a little music on the radio. I just came from there and the farm owners are sitting on the sofa in the tack room. They haven't said a word, they're just staring out the window as if they're waiting for someone to arrive."

Locket knew better than to tell Michael too much since it only gave him new ideas.

"Really?" she said. "I wonder who it might be?"

"I don't know," Michael said. "I told you, they weren't talking. I thought maybe you might know."

"No," Locket said. "Michael, if you would do me a favor and

go away, I'm waiting for someone else to show up this evening."

"Someone more important than me?" he pouted.

"Please, just this one time," Locket said. "I always talk to you when you're lonely. It's just that tonight, there might be someone else who needs to talk to me."

"Who?" he demanded.

Locket realized she'd given away too much information.

"Oh, no one, really," she answered innocently.

"Is there another ghost on this farm?" he shrieked. "This is my farm!"

"No, no," Locket said.

"I think you're lying to me!" the little ghost wailed.

"Well, fine, then," Locket said. "If that's what you think, then go look for it."

"Where?" Michael asked.

"Where what?"

"Where should I go look for it?" Michael said. "You know something! I can tell!"

"OK," Locket sighed. "If I were you, I'd check the log cabin at the top of the hill."

Michael disappeared without saying another word, and Locket felt sorry for the little family who lived in the cabin, but she knew the most he could do was turn on a few lights and maybe change the TV channel they were watching. He was a predictable ghost, which made him easier to tolerate.

"I see lights coming up the driveway!" Falstaff said and the rest of the animals moved to their stall doors and watched a large pickup truck and horse trailer slowly make its way towards the barn.

"They're here," Classy whispered.

David and Kathleen leaped to their feet and raced to the tack room door. Kathleen's heart was pounding. She had been waiting for the babies for so long and she knew she wouldn't feel they were truly safe until they were unloaded from the trailer and locked into the paddock behind the big barn.

"Hello, there!" said the truck driver as he slid down from the driver's seat. "I'm Wes. Got a special delivery for you – a mess of real pretty horses!"

"How have they been?" Kathleen asked.

"Perfect angels," the driver replied. "But then, they're pretty tired from being in the trailer for so long. We'll see how they are once they get a little sleep!"

They walked around to the back of the trailer and Kathleen stopped at a window and jumped up and down, trying to see inside.

"Hold on there, little lady," the driver said. "Give me just a minute and you'll see your new horses."

While David swung the paddock gate open, Wes unlocked the

back of the trailer and lowered the gate to the ground.

"Come on, little ones," he said. "It's time you meet your new mommy and daddy."

David and Kathleen peered into the dark trailer. Their eyes grew used to the dim light and they could just make out the shapes of the three horses slowly moving towards the open door.

"Stay back," Wes said. "They might decide to make a break for it when they get closer."

But the babies were just too tired. They walked down the ramp and one at a time stepped carefully into the paddock. David swung the gate closed and the three humans stood and stared at the little foals blinking in the bright paddock lights. One was a very small, delicate-looking appaloosa, almost all white except for a scattering of reddish brown spots. Another was a slightly larger chestnut with an unusual looking blaze on his forehead shaped like a backwards question mark. The third was the largest of them all. She was a paint and almost all white except for a brown spot on top of her head, another on her chest, and one on each side of her belly.

"Look!" Kathleen said pointing to the paint's markings. "That one has a medicine hat and a shield. And that appaloosa has a little heart-shaped spot on his hip! Oh, aren't they beautiful!"

They stood and stared at them while the three foals slowly wandered around the paddock and carefully explored their new home.

Back at the barn the other animals craned their necks and tried to see past the huge trailer.

"Can you see anything at all?" James asked. His stall was at the far end of the aisle and he had no view of the big barn.

"Not much," Classy answered. "Only the front of the truck. It's backed up to the big barn, and we can't see past it."

"The suspense is terrible," Calypso said. "I hope I have lessons tomorrow so I can meet them."

Locket leaned into the darkness, hoping to hear something. She was worried that the foals would feel alone in a new, dark and scary place and she hoped she could think of something to say to them that would make them feel better. Soon, the truck and trailer drove down the driveway and away from the farm and the paddock lights at the big barn were turned off.

Locket could barely see David and Kathleen as they wound their way down the path through the woods and back to their little house. Then, all was dark and silent. Locket sank to her knees, and then down to the ground. She decided the best thing to do was to get some sleep.

She had just closed her eyes when she heard the tiny voice again.

"Where are the mommies?" it asked. "You said there was a mommy here!"

Locket slowly lifted herself back to her feet.

"The mommy was just there," she said. "You met her."

"Noooooo!" the little voice wailed.

"Yes," Locket answered. "The lady who was just over there with you. She's the mommy. She'll take care of you."

"But she doesn't look like my mommy!" the voice replied. "I want *my* mommy!"

"Just wait a little bit," Locket said. "You'll see . . ."

"No! I don't want that kind of mommy!"

"What's you're name?" Locket asked. "Hello? What's your name?"

But there was only silence.

"You'll like this mommy! I promise!" Locket said. "Hello? Are you there?"

Locket stared at the big barn. She could hear the babies whinnying into the night.

"I know she's not your mommy," Locket said, "but if you give her a chance . . ."

"I would give her a chance," said another, deeper, larger voice. "If I could find my way there, I would give her a chance."

Chapter Ten

Babies in the barn

Locket didn't sleep at all that night. Neither voice spoke to her again and by the time the sun began to rise she was beside herself with worry.

When the sun touched Classy's face and she finally awakened, Locket told her what had happened the night before.

"Don't worry, Locket," Classy said. "They'll come around to liking it here."

"But they're so frightened!" Locket said. "And angry. Angry at me, I think!"

"No, just angry at what's happened to them," Classy said. "Don't you remember? It took you a long time to like Bethany. It was nothing like Death Valley and you were the only burro here."

"I feel like there's nothing I can do to help them," Locket said, staring off towards the big barn. "I know if I could get to them . . ."

"Ha!" Cressida said over the top of her stall door. "You never leave the paddock!"

"For something important," Locket said, "I might."

The farm house screen door squeaked and they heard David letting the yard birds out. Moments later he turned on the barn lights and began to scoop grain into buckets.

"Locket!" David said. "What's the matter? You aren't singing your breakfast song!"

Locket was so busy trying to see past the big barn she hadn't even thought about breakfast. She couldn't bring herself to feel any joy, not even for grain.

"Are you feeling OK?" he asked. "If you don't eat your breakfast, we'll get Kathleen out here to take your temperature."

"Eat!" Falstaff cautioned. "You don't want your temperature taken."

Locket ate, but she barely tasted her food. She was far too worried about the tiny, angry voice as well as the new voice, the one that sounded so hopeful, but so far away.

Kathleen joined David and together they went to the big barn. They found the three babies curled up in a heap and looking like one multi-legged, multi-colored animal. Each of them had a tiny

71

rope halter with a numbered identification tag tied to it. The same number was also glued to the hair on their backs.

"Oh, just look at them," Kathleen whispered. "They're so tiny – just little babies. The poor things are too young to be away from their mothers."

"Only four months old," David said. "How long would they usually be left with their mothers?"

"Around six months," Kathleen said. "But their mothers had to be brought back into the barn so the farmers could start collecting their urine again."

She slipped between the fence rails and stood in the paddock. The babies began to wake up and the largest one was the first to leap to her feet. She firmly planted herself in front of the other two as they slowly stood and huddled behind her.

"Isn't she the protective one," Kathleen said. "She's the one we're calling Beatrice. The little appaloosa is Benny."

"What about the chestnut?" David asked.

"We're not keeping him," Kathleen said. "Whoever adopts him can name him, don't you think?"

The two of them sat on a hay bale and stared at the foals for a long time. The little foals stared back but stayed on the other side of the small paddock. David and Kathleen pulled tufts of hay out of the bale and held them out and the two smaller babies tried to inch closer while Beatrice tried to keep them back. A little at a time the entire group of foals became more and more curious, and perhaps even hungry, and the chestnut reached out and took a nibble of hay from David's outstretched hand.

"Did you see that?" he said. "Did you see that? He likes me!"

The foal munched for a moment, then reached out to take more hay from David's hand. Then more. Soon, Benny was eating from Kathleen's hand, as well.

Beatrice, apparently disgusted with their behavior, stalked to the far corner of the paddock and glared at them.

"I guess we know who the tough one is," Kathleen said.

Cathy arrived to feed the boarders and the sound of her truck pulling into the driveway startled the babies. The boys hid behind Beatrice and Benny tried to nurse off of the filly as if she were his mother.

"Oh, the poor thing," Kathleen said. "Look how much he misses his mommy."

"Look at the pretty babies!" Cathy said as she slid out of her truck. "How cute!"

"Aren't they?" Kathleen said.

"The chestnut one likes me," David said.

"Isn't that the foster baby?" Cathy asked.

"Yes," David replied. "But he's really friendly. I don't think we'll have any trouble finding him a home at all."

The little chestnut began to inch out from behind Beatrice again and slowly walk towards David, who held out another handful of hay. The humans kept perfectly still as he approached so they wouldn't frighten him. The foal took the handful of hay, chewed on it, then looked at David as if to ask where the next handful was. When David didn't immediately grab more, the foal leaned in and placed his head on David's shoulder, nuzzling him.

David slowly reached up and placed his hand on the baby's neck and gently pet him. Then he slowly reached down and pulled another handful of hay from the bale and held it out. The foal took it in his mouth before prancing off to the far side of the paddock, very proud of himself for being so brave.

"Did you see that?" David said. "He likes me! He really likes me! How could we possibly let him go to another home?"

Kathleen and Cathy stared at him as if they'd never seen him before in their lives.

"Did you hear that?" Kathleen said. "You are my witness, Cathy. I had nothing to do with this."

"I saw it and I heard it," Cathy said, "but I don't believe it!"

"Well, he likes me!" David said.

"Yes, yes he does," Kathleen agreed, "Or at least he likes hay enough not to mind getting it from you. I'm starting to wonder just exactly how wild these babies are."

As much as they wanted to sit all day with the foals, everyone

74

had to get to work. Cathy had to feed the boarders and turn them out into their grassy pastures and David and Kathleen had to get to their offices.

The babies had never eaten grain before and didn't understand it was food, but they had to learn to eat it. They no longer had their mother's milk and hay wasn't rich enough for growing foals. Kathleen sprinkled some sweet feed over their hay and hoped they would get a few bits of it into their mouths and grow accustomed to it, while David topped off their water tank. They also put a few small pieces of carrots on the hay, but none of the foals knew how to chew anything quite that hard yet and they barely sniffed at them before pushing them aside with their noses.

"I think they'll all be just fine," Kathleen said.

"I don't know," David said. "That Beatrice looks pretty tough. She doesn't want any part of this."

He was right – Beatrice stood in the farthest corner and glared at them. She only approached the hay after they stepped far back from the paddock and she never took her narrowed, blue eyes off them.

"Well, if the chestnut really likes us," Kathleen said, "I'd have to say Miss Beatrice more than makes up for it – she's *not* happy to be here!"

"What are we going to call that boy?" David asked.

"The chestnut?" Kathleen said. "You mean, now that he's

staying?" she asked.

"Well . . ."

"I was thinking, actually, he looks like a Bart," Kathleen said.

"You know, he really does," David said. "Wassup Bart?" he called into the paddock, and the little red horse looked up at him. "OK, Bart it is!" he said.

They went back to their little house, both of them deep in thought. David was amazed at how happy he was to have made such an immediate connection with the tiny, red foal.

Kathleen, however, was dealing with a much more difficult problem. She was concerned about how she would break through to the blue-eyed paint, Beatrice, who was so angry, and yet, so sad. Also, now that David had decided the chestnut was going to stay, she didn't know how she was going to break the news to him about the dun appaloosa with the perfect blanket on his butt – the one she had reserved late the day before only seconds before David had walked in the door from work. She had thought he'd get used to the idea of a third foal while the foster was there, and by the time the foster left, he'd be able to handle the arrival of another foal to replace it. Now, however, there would be a total of four. Maybe this foal would be the one to push her husband just a little too far.

Chapter Eleven

Badly behaved babies

Percival, the young goose, was growing at an amazing rate. One day, she was slightly smaller than the white ducks, Sunny and Buttercup. The next day, she was the same size, and the day after that, she was bigger than them. No one in the yard had ever seen a bird grow at such a rapid pace and the ducks were amazed.

The crows, however, were annoyed. It took a lot of food to fill a goose growing that quickly. While the ducks would eat a little dog food and move on to look for worms and grubs, Percival rapidly ate everything in site then stood and stared at the door hoping for more.

Wilson and Carl, tired of dodging the goose they now called, "The big, fat, white vacuum cleaner," had to fight for peanuts with the rest of the morning flock. While they were unhappy with this turn of events they had learned to make a game out of it. The birds would try to see how many peanuts they could pack into their beaks and then carry up the hill where they would eat them in private away from the scurrying squirrels.

"I bet you can't carry four," Wilson said, picking up his first and second, and then scuffling with a squirrel who tried to take the third one he was eying.

"You can't carry four, either," Carl said, diving for a triple-sized peanut. "Can't even *get* four peanuts, there are so many crows on this side of the house."

"Not to mention squirrels," Wilson said as one yanked a peanut right out of his mouth and made him drop the other two. "Hey, knock it off, dude! Hit the road, you little tree rodent!"

The squirrel laughed as it ran away with the peanut in its mouth.

"Wanna go see if the big, fat white vacuum cleaner's done? Maybe she missed a few bites," Carl said.

"Yeah, what the heck," Wilson said. "This is too much like work."

The crows flew over the top of the house.

"You two stay out of trouble," Carla called after them. "Do you hear me?"

"Yes, Mom," Carl mumbled, embarrassed. None of the other mothers still kept an eye on their nearly grown offspring, but Carla was not like the other mothers – she never quit.

When they landed in the yard they found that Percival had finished off every last bite of food and stood at the door, apparently willing it to spew seconds.

"Not gonna happen, fat bird," Wilson said.

The goose still stood and stared.

"She's just a baby," Sunny said. "Don't pick on her."

"Biggest baby I ever saw," Wilson said.

"I'm still hungry," Percival said.

"Hey, me too," Carl said, "and it's your fault."

"I have an idea," Wilson said. "Those new babies at the big barn don't eat their grain. Let's go over there and clean it up for them."

The crows took off and flew through the trees to the small paddock behind the big barn where the three foals stood picking at bits of leftover hay.

"Mind if we eat some of that grain?" Carl said as they landed on the fence. "You guys aren't touching it."

"It's not for eating," Benny said.

"Then what's it for?" Wilson asked.

"I don't know," Benny said, "but it can't be food. The hay tastes kinda like grass, and Mommy said grass was good for me, so I'll just eat hay."

"So we can help ourselves?"

"Go ahead," Beatrice said, glaring. "Who cares?"

"Wow, you're a cheerful one," Carl said as he dove to the ground and started picking through the hay for grain.

Beatrice turned and walked away, and Bart and Benny followed her to a far corner.

"If I ever have an attitude like that, just smack me," Carl said.

"Don't worry, I will!" said Carla from the roof of the barn where she had just landed. "You boys are going to get in trouble over here, I just know it."

"Oh, Mom!" Carl whined.

"Eat fast, and I'll keep lookout from up here," Carla said. "I heard a fox got a young crow behind this barn just last week."

The boys rolled their eyes but ate quickly and often glanced over their shoulders. The barn backed up to a section of woods where a family of foxes lived. They often ran out and grabbed songbirds picking at leftover feed. The young crows weren't big enough yet to win a battle with a fox.

"Let's go," Carla called from the roof. "The people are on their way over!"

The crows took off, and David and Kathleen came around the corner of the barn. David was carrying a bale of hay which he tossed into the paddock. The foals started walking toward it until they saw the humans slip between the rails of the fence.

"Oh, we're gonna play that game again," Beatrice said. "Forget it, I'll wait until they're out of here to eat."

The couple sat on the bale and pulled handfuls of hay from the bale. They held them out towards the babies and sat very still.

"I'm hungry," Bart said. "They don't do anything to hurt us. I'm going over."

"Me, too," Benny said.

"Don't trust them," Beatrice said from her corner.

The boys walked towards the humans' outstretched hands and nibbled at the hay. Handful after handful, they stood munching and grabbing for more. They were so busy eating they didn't notice the hands were not reaching so far anymore, and they had to lean in closer and closer to the people to eat. At first they didn't even notice the people had hooked a rope onto each of their halters.

Bart felt a little tug on the bottom of his halter, something he'd never experienced before, and he tried to leap back but was stopped by the rope. He reared up on his hind legs, but the man pulled him down towards the ground where he froze and planted his feet, wild-eyed and confused.

Benny also felt the tug, but didn't panic until Bart leaped into

81

the air. He took three quick steps backwards and began to whip his head from side to side, trying to make the woman to let go of the rope attached to his face.

"Ha!" Beatrice said from the corner. "Told you they were up to something."

"Help!" Bart whinnied. "Help! I'm stuck!"

"Me, too!" Benny whined.

"I should just let you learn your lesson, but . . ." Beatrice shook her head, and her short, curly white mane sent shavings flying all around her. She pawed the ground a few times before she ran full speed from her corner right between the people and the foals, causing everyone to run in opposite directions. The people let go of the lead ropes and the three small horses raced to the far side of the paddock and huddled there.

"Just as I thought," Kathleen said. "We're never going to get anywhere until we separate that girl from the boys. She's taken on the role of their mommy and she's decided to protect them."

"We can work on that tonight," David said. "At least we got lead ropes on two of them. Maybe when we get them separated, we'll get one on her."

They walked back towards the house to get ready for work.

"I have an interview today," Kathleen said. "The Observer's going to run an article about the babies. I told the foal adoption group I'd help them with publicity since I know something about newspapers. We want to try to get some of the new foals adopted to this area."

"Um," David said, stopping and turning to look at her, "what did you mean by new foals?"

"Well, the adoption group agreed to take on another farm's babies," she said, not quite meeting his eyes. "There are nearly sixty more babies going up on the website. I got a sneak preview the other day."

"But we aren't getting any more, right?"

"Well, what if there are leftovers that will go to slaughter? How can I say no to them?"

"We don't have room, Kathleen," David said. "And it's too expensive to take care of them. And we both work – one of us will have to quit work and stay home if we get any more!"

"Oh, it's not that bad," Kathleen said. "Wow, did you see that Beatrice swoop in and rescue the boys today? Isn't she something?"

"Don't change the subject," David said. "Although you might think it's possible, we can't save every horse in the world."

"Well, I think I can save all the ones I'm supposed to save," Kathleen said, perhaps a bit defiantly, and she climbed the fence and dropped into the girls' paddock to give Classy a good morning hug.

"What's that supposed to mean?" David asked.

"Just what I said," she called over her shoulder.

"We can't save every horse in the world!" he said again, then muttered something about having to go to work and figure out how to make a lot more money.

Kathleen heard what he said, but ignored it. She gave Classy a kiss on the nose and headed back to the house to clean up for work. She needed to come up with a plan to tell David about the new horse and still stay married to him.

Chapter Twelve

Talking horse sense

Calypso didn't have any lessons until afternoon and she found herself wishing summer camp hadn't ended so she could go over to see the foals right after breakfast.

Locket said she hadn't heard from the babies that night, but the new voice had spoken to her again.

"He asked me how a baby could get to our farm, and I didn't know what to tell him," Locket said. "All I could think of to say was that the horses that are supposed to end up here will always find a way."

"That sounds pretty lame," Cressida said. "If I were that poor horse, I'd say you were of no help whatsoever."

"What would you have said?" Calypso asked.

"Hey," Cressida replied. "I don't have to think of what to say. I don't hear voices or see ghosts so I get to focus on important things like food and escaping. Which is something you'd actually like to do today, even though you're usually such a goody-two-shoes."

Cressida was right. Although she'd never before considered that kind of behavior, if the gate was unlatched Calypso would walk right next door and introduce herself to the babies and tell them everything was going to be just fine.

Calypso wandered towards the shed to nibble on some hay, and Locket walked over to the corner where Classy was grazing.

"Classy, I need help with something," Locket said.

"What's up?" Classy asked.

"That other horse, the one that's so far away, he kept me up all night," Locket said. "I can't talk with Cressida around, she's just too . . . well, you know how she is."

"I know," Classy said. "So what did it say?"

"It's not an it, it's a he," Locket said. "And he's as nice as can be. He told me his name and what kind of horse he is and all about his mother, who he hasn't seen in days. He's in an outside paddock with a few other babies, but sometimes, he thinks he can hear her calling to him from inside the big barn."

"What's his name?" Classy asked.

"He's Earnestly Seeking Galileo," Locket said, "but he says to just call him Ernie. He said he's a draft horse and bigger than almost all the other babies on the farm."

"Sounds like that goose over in the yard," Classy said. "I wonder if he eats as much."

"What do I do?" Locket said.

Classy knew her friend was very tired and very frightened of the responsibility she now felt for these new babies who had found a way to talk to her.

"You don't worry about it," Classy said. "I think I have a plan."

"What is it?" Locket asked, brightening.

"Let me think about it a little while," Classy said. "Why don't you go take a nap and we'll talk about it later?"

Locket sighed and walked over to a sunny spot to stretch out on the ground. She felt better having told someone, especially someone as smart as Classy. She rolled in the dust a few times before she flopped down onto her side and dozed while the name "Earnestly Seeking Galileo" danced through her mind like a sweet little melody.

Classy stared at the big barn through the woods. These babies were getting to be rather demanding, she thought, with all their comings and goings and nagging poor Locket in the middle of the night. But Classy also knew what it felt like to want to find her true home and she knew she had to find a way to help. She had an idea, but she wasn't sure she could make it work. She and Kathleen were very good at telling each other how they felt, but Classy had never before tried to tell her something as specific as a name.

By mid-afternoon, one of the barn helpers, Emily, finally arrived to bring Calypso next door for lessons. She led her through the woods towards the barn and Calypso thought about how she could get near the foals. She'd never before run away from anyone, but she needed more time than just a quick glance at them through the fence.

Halfway down the path Calypso saw there was no one else near the barn. Emily was barely holding the lead rope, which on any other day was not a problem. But Calypso was a horse with a mission. She slowed her pace so she was walking a little behind Emily, then bolted towards the barn, easily pulling the rope from the girl's hand.

"Hey!" she heard Emily shout from behind her. "Hey! Come back here! Calypso!"

Calypso was a small, old pony but she worked hard every day and was in great shape. She was at the back gate behind the barn in seconds.

Just on the other side of the fence stood the three foals,

munching on a bale of hay.

"Hi, there!" Calypso said. "Welcome to our farm! I'm Calypso."

"I'm Benny," said the smallest of the three.

"I'm Bart," said a slightly bigger chestnut.

"And I'm not impressed," said the largest one, who Calypso knew was Beatrice.

"What's the matter?" Calypso asked.

"What do you think?" Beatrice replied. "We just got dragged away from thousands of acres of beautiful pasture and all our friends and family and we're stuck in this little pen with ropes on our faces and we're supposed to be happy about it?"

"But this is your home, now," Calypso said. "You'll like it here."

"You may like it here," Beatrice said, "but no one can make me like it. I've already had enough."

"But if you just give it a chance, you'll see," Calypso said. "The owners really love all of us here, and Kathleen is a really nice mommy."

"Ha!" Beatrice said. "She can't be a mommy. No milk, no long tail to hide behind – she's no mommy!"

"Calypso!" Emily shouted as she came up next to her and grabbed her lead rope. "What was that all about? Don't you ever do that! And you have to stay away from these babies. They're in quarantine."

She dragged Calypso into the barn and began to groom her so she could saddle her for lessons.

Calypso managed to steal a few glances at the foals between afternoon lessons. The boys seemed curious about her, but Beatrice refused to look in her direction.

"That's one tough horse," she said to Classy when she returned to the barn for dinner. "I don't know how they're ever going to get her to like it here, or even be pleasant. She hates everything and everybody."

"My guess is she's just scared," Classy said. "Sometimes when you're scared it comes out as angry."

After dinner, Kathleen haltered Classy and brought her to the big barn and tacked her for their evening ride. She brushed her until she was nice and clean and put a pretty, flowered blanket on her before placing the saddle on her back. She led her outside to the mounting block which was very close to the foals' paddock.

The babies were at the fence, and Classy quickly figured out which foal was which from what Calypso had told her about them.

"Beatrice," she whispered. "Hey, Beatrice."

The white paint filly looked in Classy's direction, and for just a second, the Arab thought she saw a frightened, panicked look in the baby's blue eyes. It quickly passed and became a cold glare before Beatrice turned her back on Classy and stalked away.

"Come on, pretty girl," Kathleen said, swinging her leg over Classy's back. They were so in tune with each other's thoughts Kathleen barely had to give any direction to the mare, and the two of them rode up the hill to canter through the back fields.

Later that evening David and Kathleen sat on a bale of hay in the paddock and handed the foals little bunches of hay. Every now and then they gave a gentle tug on their lead ropes to get them used to it. Beatrice stayed far away.

After a little while, when they realized Beatrice wasn't going to come near them at all, the couple left and returned with a stack of portable fence panels. They quickly pieced together a small pen within the paddock. The foals didn't like this new activity and stayed as far away as they could, but then several more people entered the paddock. They carried blankets, and when they held them up in front of themselves they made a wall. Kathleen shooed Benny and Bart away from Beatrice, who began to panic. She ran back and forth looking for an opening to get away from the people and their wall of blankets. She finally spotted a gap and rushed through the opening . . . right into the new little pen that had just been built for her. The boys tried to follow, but David quickly slammed the gate closed, and the foals were neatly separated.

"There you go," David said to Kathleen. "Give her your best shot!"

Kathleen slipped into the pen with Beatrice. The space was so small, the foal couldn't get more than a few feet away from her in any direction.

"OK, little girl," Kathleen said. "It's about time we started to come to an understanding. I'm the mommy, you're the baby, and you're going to learn that I'm never going to hurt you. I know you're scared, but I can tell you're a very smart little baby, so it's time for you to learn your first lesson."

Beatrice turned her back to her and tucked her face into a corner of the pen, but Kathleen reached out a hand and placed it on her rump. The filly tried to move away, but no matter where she moved, Kathleen stayed right alongside her and refused to remove her hand.

"Be careful you don't get kicked!" Cathy said from the paddock. "I had a foal kick me in the face and break my nose."

"She's not a kicker," Kathleen said quietly while following Beatrice's every move. "She's a very good girl, and she's going to learn very quickly."

It was nearly thirty minutes later before Beatrice finally stopped moving away from her. She stood with her face hidden in the corner, trembling and furious that she couldn't get away from the stubborn woman who refused to take her hand off her rump.

Kathleen stood next to her and slowly rubbed her fingers through Beatrice's heavy coat. It felt really good to the little horse, and she allowed herself to relax just a little bit. In that split second, David, who was watching just outside the pen, managed to reach through the rails and snap a lead rope onto Beatrice's halter.

Beatrice reared up and spun around, furious at having let her guard down and gotten caught.

Kathleen quickly climbed over the fence and got out of the way.

"I guess that's good enough for tonight," she said. "We'll start again early tomorrow."

They tossed more hay into the paddock and Beatrice's pen, topped off the water buckets, and left for the night.

Beatrice huddled in a corner, and the boys leaned up against her through the fence. She couldn't believe what had become of her life – it had all been so perfect for so long. She closed her eyes, feeling lost in her loneliness, and remembered what it was like to race through huge, open green meadows at her mother's side, surrounded by a hundred other foals.

"She's getting there," Kathleen said to David as they got ready for bed. "She'll come around."

"She seems like she might be a little dangerous," David said. "You have to be more careful."

"No, she's just frightened," Kathleen replied. "She'll be OK. You'll see."

"OK, but promise you won't go over there and work with her

without me," David said.

"I think I can take care of myself," Kathleen replied. "I don't need a baby sitter."

"Just promise me you won't go over alone," he said again.

"Fine," she said.

Kathleen opened the bedroom window so she could hear the noises of the farm, and she climbed into bed next to David. She thought about the frightened filly and tried to remember everything she'd ever learned about horses. Maybe there was something she had forgotten that would help her get through to this baby.

David turned off the lights, and Kathleen closed her eyes. She tried to imagine how the foals felt, with no mothers, no milk, no green grass. She pictured a herd of young foals and their mothers, quietly grazing in an endless pasture. She could see them so clearly, all colors and shapes and sizes. Some babies were nursing from their mothers while others nibbled at the grass and tried to figure out why their mothers seemed to love it so much. Sometimes the babies bolted and ran, chasing each other across the field then quickly returning to their mothers. They had no idea how their world would change, and they certainly didn't know their fate might be a terrible death.

As Kathleen imagined the scene, it seemed that one very large foal in the herd was trying to get her attention. She focused on it, and all the other horses faded into the background. It was a very tall, long-legged, deep brown horse with three fluffy, white feathered feet and a crooked blaze on its forehead. Then she heard a voice that was so clear and loud her eyes flew open and she sat up and reached over to turn on the lamp.

"What's the matter?" David said, rolling over and propping himself up on one elbow.

"Did you hear that?" Kathleen asked him.

"Hear what?"

"That voice!"

"Nope," he said, rolling back over. "Maybe it was that pesky ghost again."

Kathleen sank back into her pillow, but waited a few minutes before she turned the light off. She was sure she had heard a voice, familiar but strange, as clearly as if someone was standing next to the bed. It had said, "His name is Earnestly Seeking Galileo."

Chapter Thirteen

A lonely little filly

Kathleen and Classy both loved September. They rode the trails and quiet country roads of Bethany and paused to sniff at pockets of early autumn smells. The air was rich with the scent of ripe wild purple grapes that dropped to the ground with soft thuds as horse and rider wound their way beneath the heavy vines. Farmers were busily harvesting the last of their hay and spreading it out in long rows where it would turn golden-yellow beneath the slanting sunlight. Drying corn stalks rattled in the breeze and squirrels raced back and forth from woods to fields carrying impossibly large black walnuts locked within lumpy, green cases.

The daisies in the wildflower gardens pushed their eager faces towards the sun, soaking up the last bits of warmth before the frost arrived and curled them into dark bundles of seed. They would burst with November's cold, stiff wind, scattering them to the earth where they would root with early spring rains.

A fat gopher nibbled on ripe tomatoes and peppers in the vegetable garden and the paint pony, Cressida, as well as the goats, Doc and Ezzie, longed to escape and feast on the apples and pears lying on the ground beneath the trees.

Duck took a few nibbles at a pear as he waddled his way over to the parrot's window. The weather would change soon and the window would be closed for the winter so Duck would lose contact with the house birds until the winds blew warm again in the spring.

"Hey, bird!" Duck called in the window. "Wassup?"

Polonius was standing on top of her cage, eyes glued to something Duck couldn't see.

"Not now, Duck," Polonius said. "We're watching Animal Court and Judge Wopner's about to make a decision."

Duck poked through the piles of empty peanut shells while he waited. A minute later, he heard the birds cheering wildly, obviously approving of the judge's verdict.

"OK, Duck," Polonius said. "The pig has to leave the suburbs and go to the country where he belongs. That's one smart judge. Imagine, a full-grown pig in a tiny back yard! Phew!"

"Whatever," Duck said. "Has Kathleen told David yet?"

"About what?"

"About the new foal!" Duck said. "You know, the one with the spotted blanket on his butt."

"Oh, no," Polonius said. "Not yet. She was talking to a friend on the phone this morning and she told her she'd break the news to him soon. Which would be a good idea since the horses are supposed to arrive within the next two weeks."

"They have to be carrotined, too, huh?"

"Quarantined, yes," Polonius sighed. "But by the time they get here, the others will be out of quarantine."

Duck peered through the window, trying to see what the rest of the birds were doing.

"Don't you guys get bored being in there all day?" he asked.

"Hardly," Polonius replied.

"Well, what do you do aside from watch TV?"

"Duck, I run the entire household from this room," Polonius said. "Now, if you'll excuse me, the next case is coming up."

"Hey, wait!" Duck said. "One more thing – have they decided what to do with Beatrice?"

"No," Polonius said, "but David's trying to convince Kathleen to send her out for training. She'll have nothing to do with it, but I think she's getting tired, as she should. I've heard what goes on over there."

"Hey, by the way," Duck said. "How'd you get out of that cage?"

"Michael opened the door," Polonius replied.

"That ghost sure gets around," Duck said.

Polonius turned her back, and Duck waddled towards the paddock. From everything he had heard, Beatrice was a lost cause. While Bart and Benny had come around very quickly, allowing David and Kathleen to brush them all over, pick up their feet and even hold their lead ropes without a problem, Beatrice was still angry and sullen. Kathleen was able to box her into a corner and pet her, but the filly never let her guard down and as soon as she saw an opportunity to move away from Kathleen, she took it. Beatrice also refused to behave when her lead rope was held, pulling and bucking and twisting, even though Kathleen always held on tight. After each long, exhausting battle, Beatrice would finally give up and stand with her face tucked in a corner, chest heaving from the struggle, her coat drenched in sweat.

Kathleen was no better off. She'd wipe the sweat from her face with the sleeve of her flannel shirt, keeping a hand on Beatrice at all times and never letting go of the rope, knowing if she lost her concentration, the filly would notice and start to twist and buck. David always stood just outside the fence, terrified Kathleen was going to get hurt.

"You can't keep doing this," he'd say.

99

"I'll keep doing this as long as I have to," she'd answer through clenched teeth as she clung to the lead rope.

David knew how stubborn his wife was, and that keeping her out of Beatrice's pen would require tying her down with lots of rope and duct tape, so he kept careful watch and waited outside the fence in case he had to dive through and save her.

The tension was growing, and the entire farm could feel it, including Duck. It seemed with each passing day of battling with Beatrice he got less and less attention from David and Kathleen. And with Bo away at college, he was feeling a little neglected.

"Duck!" Cressida called to him from the paddock. "Grab me a pear on the way up, will you?"

Duck grabbed the stem of a small, green pear and lugged it to the paddock where he dropped it in front of the pony as he squeezed under the fence.

"You'll get a tummy ache," Calypso warned Cressida.

"I will not, and it's none of your business," Cressida replied as she grabbed the pear and crunched it to bits between her strong teeth.

"If you're making deliveries, we'd like to put in an order," Doc said. She sniffed the ground beneath where the fat pony had chewed the pear and searched for tidbits.

"Not today, goat," Duck replied. "I'm here on business. The house bird just told me something I thought you might be

100

interested in."

"What is it, Duck?" Locket said. Her tall ears perked up.

"David is trying to get Kathleen to send Beatrice out for training," Duck said. "Oh, and she still didn't tell him about the new foal."

"But he knows about the new boarder foal," Locket said, "and he's fine with that."

After the article appeared in the newspaper, a Bethany woman named Brendee had decided to adopt a PMU colt and board him at Locket's Meadow until she could build a barn in her backyard.

"He says that foal won't cost him any money," Duck said, "so it's OK. Also, it's not supposed to stay here very long."

"They would send that filly out to be trained?" Classy said. "I've never heard of them doing anything like that."

"Kathleen won't let it happen," Calypso said.

"But what if Kathleen gets hurt?" Classy said. "What if that crazy filly tramples her? What would we do then? Maybe she *should* go away."

"Have you heard from any of the foals lately?" Duck asked Locket.

"Just Ernie," she said. "We talk every night. But not a word from the baby at the big barn, whichever one it was."

Locket still wasn't sure which of the babies had talked to her those first few nights.

"No one who comes here ever gets sent away, for training or anything else," Locket said.

"Hey, I go to horse shows!" Falstaff said, leaning over the fence.

"But you come back home the same day," Classy said. "It's different. Training can take months."

"That's just not the way it's done on this farm," Locket said. "The day it happens, none of us will feel safe. We have to do something about it."

While the animals stood in the paddock trying to figure out how to get Beatrice to behave, Kathleen sat at the desk in her office thinking about the same thing. She was tired and her arms hurt from wrestling the 300 pound filly. Her fingers were so sore from holding the lead rope, she could hardly type her stories.

She had tried everything she could think of to get Beatrice to trust her but nothing was working. Kathleen knew David would not be able to watch the battle for much longer. With another foal coming soon she needed to get the ones they had under control before she could even think about telling her husband about a new one.

And, to make matters even worse, she had become obsessed with the name Earnestly Seeking Galileo. She heard it at the oddest times, echoing endlessly in her head. She thought it might be the name of a very large, very quiet horse, but she had no idea who he was or where he could possibly be. The only thing she knew for sure was it wasn't the dun colored appaloosa with the perfect blanket on his butt, the one she had managed to keep a secret from her husband. That one was scheduled to arrive within the next few weeks. She hoped for David's sake that Earnestly Seeking Galileo was only a figment of her very vivid imagination.

The phone rang and she picked it up with her swollen fingers.

"The Weekly News, Kathleen speaking."

"Hi, darling," David said. "It's me."

"Hi! What's up?"

"Do you want to meet me for lunch?" David asked.

"I can't," Kathleen replied. "I have so much to do and I can't seem to concentrate."

"All right," David said. "But I wanted to talk to you about Beatrice. I've called several trainers and I think I've found one who'll be able to get her to calm down. I think we should consider sending her there for a few months."

"Absolutely not!" Kathleen said. "I can figure this horse out."

"Don't you think you would have by now if you could?" David answered as gently as he could. "She's too tough, and you're going to get hurt."

"I will not!" she replied.

"Kathleen, you're so tired you can hardly get out of bed in the morning. Your parrots are feeling neglected, and frankly, so am I. Are we ever going to go out to dinner or to a movie again? All you ever think about anymore is how to get Beatrice gentled."

Kathleen didn't answer right away. She knew he was right about all of her attention going to Beatrice but she wasn't ready to give up. She thought about how frightened and angry the little filly was and how badly she needed to trust someone and allow them to love her. Even the best trainer would be a stranger to Beatrice, and moving her to yet another new place would be more frightening.

"Give me a little more time, David," Kathleen said. "I have an idea. If I can't get through to her in the next few days, we can talk about a trainer."

"It's a deal," David replied sounding very relieved. "Do you want me to bring you a salad to eat at your desk?"

"Sure," she said. She tried to sound cheerful despite being overwhelmed by the task of making a wild horse gentle, telling her husband about the new appaloosa with the perfect blanket on his butt, and that the name Earnestly Seeking Galileo had just popped into her head once again as it did many times every day.

"Knock it off!" she said out loud to the voice as she hung up the phone and several people in the office turned and stared at her.

At the same time Locket was also lost in thought. She paced

in her paddock trying to think of a way to help Beatrice. She understood what it was like to be in a strange place, afraid of new sounds, smells and people. She had been snatched up from Death Valley in late summer and was used to hot days and feeding on dry, tough plants and scrub brush. She arrived in Connecticut in the autumn, frightened and shivering in the cold nights. Her only experience with people had been horrible and painful and frightening, and there she was, surrounded by them, each one trying to touch her any chance they could. She expected them to poke her with sharp needles, push her back onto a dark trailer and send her far away again. It was a long time before she learned to trust humans and longer still before she understood she was now safe and had escaped death by coming here.

Locket thought if she could talk to Beatrice she could convince her that this farm was a good, safe place. But how? The little voice had not spoken to her in weeks.

Locket stared through the woods at the big barn. She knew a sad and lonely young filly lived on the other side of it and if she didn't learn how to behave soon she might never finish her quarantine and come home to the little barn. Despite the fact that Locket had not left her paddock since she had arrived years ago, she realized the only way she could reach Beatrice was by escaping and walking over for a visit.

Chapter Fourteen

In the dark of night

When Locket announced she was going to visit the foals that night the paddock erupted in protest.

"Let Cressida go next door," Classy said. "She knows how to get loose and she has no problem leaving the paddock."

"Yes, of course," Locket said, rather crossly. "Cressida's great at cheering up other animals. She's just what Beatrice needs."

"Well, then, I'll go," Classy said. "I go to the big barn all the time. I can talk to her."

"Or I can go," Calypso said. "I could walk that path with my eyes closed."

"No," Locket said. "I've already experienced what she's going through, and I know exactly how she feels. She doesn't understand that she would have been killed if she hadn't come here and that Kathleen is only trying to help her."

"How are you going to break out?" Cressida asked. "Break down the fence, maybe?"

"No!" Locket said, appalled.

"Hey, Locket!" Duck said. "You want company? I'll go with you."

"You can't," Locket said. "They lock you in before dark, and I have to do this at night."

"And it's dangerous for a duck to walk through the woods at night," the old rooster said from the chicken pen. "There are foxes and coyotes and raccoons and they're all hungry."

"I'll be fine," Duck said. "And I have a brilliant idea."

"What is it?" Locket asked. She thought of everyone on the farm, the one she would most like to keep her company on her mission was Duck.

"Tell us about it," Classy said, and all the animals leaned in close to Duck and listened.

Most evenings, Michael visited the barn just after dark. It was a little lonely being a ghost that no one could see except for one little burro which is why he liked to stir up so much trouble. That way at least *someone* noticed he existed.

107

That evening he stopped to visit Locket and tell her the list of pranks he had planned for that evening, but Locket interrupted him.

"So," she said, "the duck tells me you know how to open the house bird cages?"

"Easy peasy," Michael said. "Simplest form of lock opening there is. One little push and they're sprung."

"I find that hard to believe," Locket said. "I think it would take a very clever ghost to turn a parrot loose."

"Are you suggesting I'm not clever?"

"No, no, not at all," Locket said. "I'm just saying that I think there's a certain amount of *talent* involved in that kind of jailbreak that maybe a ghost wouldn't be capable of."

"I can open anything!" Michael growled, glowing with indignation.

"Could you open Duck's cage?" Locket asked.

"Ha!" the little ghost sneered. "Not even a challenge!"

"Duck says it's a hook and eye," Locket said. "I find it hard to believe you could lift and open something as secure as that."

"Listen, burro," Michael said, puffing himself up to almost twice his size. "If I say I can do it, I can do it. As a matter of fact, I'm heading over there to open his cage right this second."

And Michael quickly deflated and slipped towards the barn door.

"Hey, wait!" Locket said. "How will I know *you* did it?"

Michael floated back towards Locket.

"Duck will tell you, you silly animal," he said.

"But how will I know for sure it was *you*?" Locket said. "Duck can't see you and I've heard rumors of other ghosts lurking about the farm. You could ask *them* to do it for you."

"What other ghost? There is no other ghost on my farm!" Michael said. He was so angry the air around him turned white with frost. "I'm the only one!"

"Yes, of course," Locket said.

"Don't believe me?"

"I don't believe you have the talent for that kind of lock, Michael," Locket said. "I'd have to see it with my own eyes, I suppose."

"Well, you won't leave the paddock," he said.

"I might, if someone opened the gate for me," Locket said. "It wasn't so many years ago I wandered around the entire Death Valley wilderness. I could walk from the paddock to the yard."

Without hesitating, Michael unlatched Locket's gate, which only had one lock. Even when he'd opened it in the past the girl's never bothered to walk through the open door. Both of them were usually quite content to stay inside.

The door swung open in the dim light, and Locket took a step towards it.

"You can do it," Calypso whispered from her stall.

Classy gave Locket a little nudge with the tip of her nose.

"It'll be fun," Classy said. "An adventure."

"Bring me back a pear," Cressida said.

Locket closed her eyes for a moment and thought about the sad and angry little horse next door. She remembered her own first days in Connecticut and how miserable she had been. She thought about her own mother, who had disappeared long before Locket had been captured and how lonely she had been until she learned to love her new home. Then, she opened her eyes and stepped through the gate.

"Come on, burro," Michael was saying. "Don't think I can open a duck cage, huh? I'll show you."

Locket walked through the barn, past the ponies and Falstaff and James, who stared at her as if *she* was the ghost.

"Whooooah!" James said. "Never thought I'd see the day!"

"Neither did I," Falstaff said.

"Well, you thought wrong, now, didn't you," Locket said as she slowly walked past, carefully placing one dainty foot in front of the other.

She emerged from the barn into pale moonlight. Behind the little pond and nestled against the side of the house sat the duck pens. The kitchen lights were on but Locket didn't see anyone moving inside. She had heard the car leave earlier that evening and she hoped whoever had gone out would stay away for a while longer.

"It's the first cage," Locket said, determinedly placing one foot in front of the other.

"I know which one is Duck's!" Michael hissed.

He drifted right through the fence and stopped in front of Duck's cage.

"It's a simple focus and lift procedure," he said. "I've done plenty like this. It's no harder than a light switch, really."

"Really," said Locket, trying to keep her voice steady. She was trembling from the tip of her nose to her tail. "So, let's see this talent of yours."

Michael crouched in front of the cage and focused.

POP! The hook leaped out of the eye and Duck nudged the door open.

"That's incredible!" Locket said. "I never would have believed you could do it. Well, you proved me wrong, didn't you!"

The ghost puffed up to nearly double his size.

"Won't doubt me again, will you?" he said.

"No, Michael, never again!" Locket said.

"If you'll excuse me, I have to get back to my regularly scheduled evening activities," he said. "I'm a little behind on my agenda."

And Michael evaporated into the night.

Duck slipped out of his cage and flapped his wings as he ran across the yard. He leaped into the air and soared over the fence, landing with a thump next to Locket.

"Well, look at you!" he whispered. "You OK?"

"I think so," Locket replied. "Let's get going before someone comes home."

Chapter Fifteen

If burros had wings

Kathleen had told David she couldn't work with the foals that evening because she had a meeting to attend. It was the first time she had ever told him a lie. Her real plan was to go right to the foals' paddock and work with Beatrice without David hovering around the pen making her nervous and telling her to give up. Kathleen had no intention of letting the filly go out to a trainer or any place else and she was determined to figure out how to get through to her before the end of that evening.

Kathleen left in the car and drove down the street, then turned around and returned to the farm, taking the second driveway up to the big barn. No one was there, and Kathleen switched on one small light behind the barn. Benny and Bart looked up from their hay, saw who it was, and settled back down to eating. Beatrice, who had been left in her own small pen, also looked up to see who was there. She immediately backed her rump into a corner as far away from Kathleen as she could get, keeping her head low to the ground and not allowing her angry blue eyes to waver from Kathleen's face.

"OK, Miss Bea," Kathleen said. "We're gonna work this out tonight if it's the last thing we do. Are you ready?" she said, slipping through the bars of the pen. "I know you're tough, but I think I'm tougher."

Beatrice turned around and tucked her face into the corner so Kathleen couldn't get hold of her lead line.

"I'll get it whether you want me to or not, little girl," Kathleen said, placing her hand on the filly's rump. Beatrice began moving away, and Kathleen followed, refusing to take her hand off of her no matter how quickly the horse lunged from one side of the little pen to the other. It seemed to take forever but it was only a few minutes before Kathleen was able to grab the end of the lead rope- and then the horse got really angry. She tossed her head from side to side, wild-eyed and desperate, several times dragging her captor to the ground. Each time, Kathleen leaped to her feet, just barely avoiding the horse's stomping hooves. Soon she was able to get her hand firmly on Beatrice's back while still keeping hold of the lead rope.

Both of them were out of breath and sweaty when Beatrice finally paused a moment, head tucked into her corner, regrouping for the next round.

"Here's the deal, Miss Beatrice," Kathleen said between gasps for air. "We only have one chance left to get this right before you'll have to leave, and I'm not quitting until I get through to you."

On the other side of the wooded path, Locket and Duck had cut back through the barn and were inching their way along the paddock, clinging close to the security of the fence. Duck stayed close to Locket's front feet, chatting quietly to distract her from her nerves.

"How ya doing, Locket?" Duck asked, feeling rather nervous himself.

"I've been better," Locket said, "but I've been worse."

"Yes, me too," Duck replied. "What do you think it is about leaving the paddock that bothers you so much?" he asked.

Locket had thought about this many times before.

"I think it's the unknown," she said. "I remember when I was on my way here on the trailer and each time a donkey or a burro got off, I was so afraid for them because I didn't know where they were going. And then we got here, and I was afraid for me. You know, we have a really nice paddock and really nice friends there. For me, there's no reason to leave."

"Until now," Duck said.

"Until now," Locket repeated.

They reached the end of the paddock fence, and Locket hesitated before stepping away and onto the path through the woods. The moon was bright, but the trees blocked much of the light from the soft ground. The pair was about to enter the darkest section of the farm.

"Tell me about your mother," Duck said, stepping out onto the path. "Do you remember her?"

Locket took a step after him.

"I remember her," Locket said. "It was a long time ago, but I remember her."

"Do you look like her?"

"I wish I did," Locket said, taking another step. "She was very beautiful."

"Then I'd say you look like her," Duck replied, inching slowly forward. "What happened to her? Did she get rounded up and sent away?"

"I don't know for sure," Locket said. "I know one day we were

116

out with the rest of the herd and we saw this huge, loud metal bird in the sky. It came straight down at us, and we were so frightened we began to run. We took off in different directions. I thought I was in the same group with my mother. The bird followed a different group, and there were a lot of loud noises and bangs. I looked everywhere for her but I never saw her again."

"I'm sorry," Duck said.

"What about your mother?" Locket asked.

"I don't remember her at all, really," he said. "I remember hatching and I remember being hungry and looking for something to eat. Then I remember Bo catching me and bringing me here to the kitchen. She was my real mother, I think."

Just then the pair heard the crack of a branch trampled underfoot. They froze.

"Who is it?" whispered Duck.

There was no response, but a coyote howled in the back pasture. Another branch snapped, this time much closer.

"Don't move, Duck," Locket said. "Stay right next to me."

"Ready for the next go-round, Miss Bea?" Kathleen asked after catching her breath.

She began to rub Beatrice's back where her hand rested just above her tail. Instead of backing away, the horse tucked her nose further down into the corner.

"I know you're really, really mad," Kathleen whispered, massaging the filly's back, slowly moving her hand up her spine. "And I know you're just a little baby girl who wants her mommy really bad. And here you are, with these two boys latching onto you and pretending you're their mommy, and you are *such* a good girl you decided to protect and take care of them even though all you really wanted was your own mommy."

Kathleen kept rubbing Bea's back, moving her hand closer to the horse's shoulder, and the filly's head sank even nearer to the ground.

"I have some news for you, Miss Bea," Kathleen said. "You don't have to be anyone's mommy, at least not yet. You can just be a little girl who is very lonely and sad and wishing her life hadn't gone quite this way. It's OK to want things to be different, and it's OK to be angry. It's OK to think about the way things were. But someday, when it doesn't hurt so badly, I want you to think about maybe liking me a little bit. I think we could have a nice life together, Miss Bea. I really do. We have some nice pastures and trails and fields, and next door, there are lots of other girls you can get to know. We would love a chance to be your friends."

Beatrice took a deep breath and let it out in a huge sigh. Kathleen had worked her way up to the horse's shoulder, closer to her face than she had ever gotten before.

118

Locket and Duck were about halfway down the path, still frozen in their tracks.

"What do we do?" Duck asked.

He knew that he was the one a hungry nighttime prowler would be after.

"Just don't move," Locket said.

She took a step to the side so Duck was protected between her two front feet.

"Just don't move," she said again.

Locket's tall ears turned in all directions, trying to pinpoint exactly where the noise was coming from. She heard soft, slow padding on the ground behind her, coming closer and closer.

"Locket?" Duck said, voice trembling.

"Just don't move," Locket said yet one more time.

Seconds later, a twig snapped almost directly behind them, and Locket planted her front feet solidly into the ground and let her hind legs fly in a huge kick.

A coyote flew through the air with a tremendous yelp and a second one raced towards Locket, growling. Locket braced herself and let her legs fly again, sending the animal flying smack into a tree. It squealed and took off, followed by the first coyote.

Locket and Duck stood frozen in place, listening for more, but all they could hear was the pounding of their own hearts.

"Are they gone?" Duck asked.

119

"For now," Locket said after listening carefully. "Maybe you should fly up onto my back. You'll be safer there."

"I can't move yet," Duck said.

"As soon as you're ready," Locket said, her ears rapidly twitching in all directions. "Take your time."

She was no longer afraid, at least not for herself.

"How'd you know how to do that?" Duck asked.

"We had coyotes in Death Valley," she replied. "It's a skill you never forget."

David was pacing around the house trying to think of things to do to keep busy until Kathleen got home. He had tried to read but nothing held his attention. He decided to clean the newspaper out of the bottom of the parrot cages. He felt guilty about telling Kathleen she had to send Beatrice away for training and he wanted to do something helpful.

When he was done cleaning the cages he stuffed the dirty newspaper into a garbage bag and carried it out to the garage. On his way back to the house he could see in the dim light from the back porch that Duck's cage was wide open and the big bird was nowhere in sight. He heard a coyote howl in one of the back pastures and he ran into the house to get a flashlight.

Duck feet aren't made for perching. While Wiggy could

tightly curl his rooster toes and grip Locket's hair for a secure ride, Duck's flat feet couldn't get hold of her smooth coat. It took a few steps and a lot of wobbling before he learned the easiest way to balance was by standing on Locket's shoulders with his wings fully opened, occasionally flapping them to keep his balance. The two of them looked like a winged burro warming up for takeoff.

"Almost there, Duck," Locket whispered as they emerged from the path into the field alongside the indoor riding arena. "Almost there."

Duck balanced carefully, wings spread wide. The pair hurried past the arena and along the side of the barn. They noticed a soft glow behind the barn and Locket peered around the corner of the building. Duck stretched his neck out and looked as well.

Kathleen was kneeling in front of a young paint filly, gently holding her lead rope. The two of them were eye to eye and Beatrice's blue eyes were filled with tears that welled up then softly dropping onto the matted hay beneath her. Kathleen was also crying, but she was smiling.

"That's a good girl," she said to the horse. "That's a good girl. You just be a little baby girl for as long as you want. You don't have to grow up until you feel like it. And you can be sad for as long as you need to."

She leaned over and gently kissed Beatrice on her pink nose and the wild filly stood perfectly still and let her.

Locket took a step backwards.

"I don't think they need us anymore," she whispered.

She turned to walk back towards the woods but froze again when all the paddock lights blazed to life.

David stepped out of the barn and came face-to-face with what appeared to be a short, oddly-shaped Pegasus. He then thought he had come across a winged burro, flight feathers spread and wildly flapping at its shoulders as if the creature was about to take flight. He shook his head hard, and looked again. This time he also saw the head of a duck, Mohawk hairdo fully erect, peering at him from between two tall, fuzzy ears.

"Locket?" he gasped in surprise. "What the . . . hey, wait a minute! Duck! There you are! What's going on here?"

Kathleen popped out from behind the barn.

"David?" she said, then gasped and said, "Locket? DUCK?! David, what are you doing here?"

"Kathleen, what are *you* doing here?" David demanded. "Duck! What on earth are *you* doing here?"

Duck, who had been flapping wildly to stay on Locket's back, lost his balance and flew across the driveway into the field. David and Kathleen raced behind him, trying to grab him before he got too far away.

"Locket?" the burro heard a tiny, sad voice say. "Is that you?"

122

"Yes," Locket replied, stepping forward and peering around the corner of the barn again.

"Hello," said the paint filly, looking up at the burro through blue eyes that were bright with tears. "I'm Beatrice."

Chapter Sixteen

Cressida's secret

Duck was grounded. After his late-night adventure, David and Kathleen took him home and clipped his flight feathers and now he stood quietly in the yard staring through the picket fence which now seemed like prison bars.

"Might as well be a parrot," he muttered.

The hens, whom he had so often teased because they couldn't get out of their pen, giggled and called out in unison, "Don't you wish you could *fly*, Duck!"

"I *hate* hens," Duck said.

Several weeks had passed, and things had grown quiet. Once the commotion had settled down after the "flying burro" had been caught at the barn, Locket had calmly walked back to the paddock alongside David and Kathleen, who clutched Duck tightly under her arm. David locked the burro in her pen with Classy and went directly to the garage to get a second lock which he installed on their gate. He also put a second lock on Duck's door before they went to bed that night.

Kathleen and David never figured out how Locket and Duck got to the big barn that evening and in the end they decided since everyone returned home safely, and Beatrice had begun a complete turnaround that night, they would put it behind them and hope it never happened again. However, each night they very carefully checked to make sure all the double locks were fastened before turning out the lights.

September ended and the wild grapes lay scattered and decaying on the ground, smelling faintly like red wine. After each cool October night the sun rose and lit new patches of red, yellow and orange leaves that had appeared on the trees during the night. Most of the flowers in the yard had died and folded to the ground except for the potted mums and a few bright pink zinnias. Percival the goose had grown to enormous proportions and now dwarfed Duck who until then had been the largest in the flock of Locket's Meadow yard birds.

The three foals finished their quarantine and moved to a new paddock David built next to the girls' paddock. They had a new three-sided shed to keep them warm and dry and they were learning to follow David and Kathleen on walks around the farm.

Beatrice was the quickest one to learn new things. She learned to come when Kathleen called her name and she loved having her coat brushed and her mane and tail combed. She also learned to lift her feet so they could be cleaned out with a hoof pick and she was beginning to look forward to her bucket of grain each morning.

Beatrice still thought about her mother and the endless green fields of Canada, but with each passing day, she thought less about her former life and more about her new one. She had even begun to appreciate carrots and nibbled at tiny pieces Kathleen broke off with her own teeth and fed to her.

The foals and the girls quickly made friends over their fence and within a few days it felt as if they had always known each other. For Locket, having them there was a relief. She felt responsible for them, especially Beatrice, with whom she had become wonderful friends. Yet, she was still overwhelmed with worry about the horse named Earnestly Seeking Galileo. She heard from him almost every night and he told her about his life in the far north. It had already snowed where he lived but he said his coat was heavy and kept him nice and warm. He lived in a small paddock lined up side-by-side with other paddocks which each held several large foals. He no longer heard his mother call to him from the barn, except in his dreams, and when he awoke from those dreams and was sad he called out to Locket. Ernie said she was the only one he could talk to who understood him.

Kathleen told David about the appaloosa with the perfect spotted blanket on his butt shortly after the night of the "flying burro." She explained how she reserved him when she thought they were going to place Bart in another home. When David told her he wanted to keep Bart it was already too late. David said he would deal with the newest foal, but Kathleen had to promise not to look at any new pictures of foals on-line no matter how much she wanted to. Kathleen agreed, because even she knew they were busy enough. Three foals were plenty for any farm.

Everyone settled in and waited for the new foal and the boarder foal to arrive, but each time they were given a delivery date they would soon receive a phone call saying it had been delayed. Once a huge Canadian snow storm had kept them from loading the foals and a second time a truck broke down and the hauling company needed a week to get it repaired.

"It's taking forever for those foals to get here," Locket said late one brilliant October afternoon.

The sun was bright but slanted at a sharp, faraway angle so the air never quite felt warm. The outside animals had begun to grow thick coats and Locket's was already several inches long.

"We won't find out when they're coming, anyway," said Calypso. "The windows are shut on the house and even if they

127

were open, Duck can't get over the fence to tell us anything."

"What difference does it make?" Beatrice said. "One foal will live in the boarder barn, and the other isn't going to stay."

"That's what Kathleen said," Calypso said, "but you wait and see. No one who comes to Locket's Meadow ever leaves."

Cressida rolled her eyes.

"Don't be quite so sentimental," she said. "There's always a first time. Sooner or later, they're going to run out of room."

"They will always find a way," Classy said. "You'll see."

"Cressie, how long have you lived here?" Beatrice asked.

"Three years," Cressida said.

"Where did you live before?" Beatrice asked.

"Someplace else," Cressida replied, and turned her back.

"Did you miss your mommy when you left?" Beatrice asked.

The rest of the animals watched carefully. Cressida never spoke about where she came from and if anyone asked her she told them to mind their own business. But for some reason the fat paint pony seemed to have a soft spot for Beatrice.

"I wasn't with my mother at the last place I lived," Cressida said and walked away from the rest of the horses.

Beatrice followed Cressida along the fence. She stopped next to her and stood quietly. Although Beatrice was just a young foal she was already a little taller than the pony. Their coloring was very similar and when they stood side-by-side they looked almost like sisters.

"Who is it that you miss so much?" Beatrice asked.

Cressida stood quietly and Beatrice waited patiently.

"They ran out of room at the farm," Cressida finally replied. "They needed a stall for a horse who knew how to 'really work'. They sold me and kept . . . my daughter."

The pony turned to look at Beatrice.

"She looked a little like you," Cressida said. "She had a medicine hat and a shield and bright blue eyes."

Beatrice nodded.

"Cressie," she said. "I've just learned that it's possible to have two mommies. Maybe it would be OK for you to have two daughters. I can be the one who stays forever."

Cressida looked at Beatrice through watery blue eyes.

"I wonder sometimes if she remembers me," Cressida said.

"I promise you," Beatrice said, "she always remembers you."

"Hey! Hey, dudes!" Wilson called out, flying in and landing on the fence between the girls and the babies. "I just got some news from the jail bird!"

"How?" Calypso asked as Carl landed beside Wilson. "The windows are closed."

"David burned some toast and they tossed it out to us and then opened the windows to let the smoke out," Wilson said. "And then the jail bird called me over. She said to tell you the trailer was loaded this morning and the horses are on their way."

"Carl! Wilson!" Carla called from the tall pine tree.

"Aw, geeeez," Carl said, then called out, "We're right here!"

"What did I tell you?" Carla said as she landed on the fence. "Oh, excuse me, ladies!" she said to the horses, goats and burro. "These two are both grounded. They nearly got killed in one of the back pastures teasing some young foxes. They are not allowed to fly out of my sight! You come back to the tree this instant! I have half a mind to clip all your flight feathers and leave you in the yard with that troublesome duck!"

"At least we'd get fed," Carl mumbled as he and Wilson followed his mother across the yard.

Kathleen was working at home that day. She stared out the window and watched a group of three crows fly from the paddock fence up into the pine tree. She wasn't getting very much work done. The phone call had come announcing the new foals would arrive soon, but she didn't get excited. She knew she couldn't get attached to the appaloosa since he couldn't stay on the farm, although she thought he was one of the prettiest little horses she had ever seen.

She decided just this once to take a peek at the website where all the photos of the foals were posted. She typed in the web address and watched as a short message in large, bold letters popped up as the page loaded onto the screen.

"Only two weeks left for these draft foals" it said. Below the message was a photo of a foal and Kathleen clicked on it. A dozen photos of foals, all of them huge shires, looked back at her through long eyelashes. All of them were marked "reserved" or "adopted," except for one.

Kathleen stared hard at the photo. The words beneath the horse said he had a hernia, a condition which would require surgery. Kathleen knew it would be expensive and only a crazy person would adopt a horse in that condition and bring it home and spend a huge amount of money on vet bills. She clicked on the foal's picture to enlarge it and took a closer look.

"Oh, no," she said. "Oh, please, no!"

Chapter Seventeen

A gang of two

"You know, David," Kathleen said, "if we ever got a big draft horse, wouldn't Earnestly Seeking Galileo be a perfect name for it?"

She was stirring a pot of sauce on the stove.

"Yes, that would be a great name," David replied. "*If* we were to get a big draft horse, which we are *never* going to do."

"Right! Of course not," she said. "But wouldn't that be a great name?"

"What are you up to?" David asked.

"Oh, nothing," Kathleen replied. "Do you want a little red wine with your dinner?"

"We can't get another horse, Kathleen."

"Right," she said. "I know that. You think I don't know that?"

"I think you don't know that," David said.

"David, I don't have any more time in my day!" Kathleen said. "I have enough to do with work and all the foals we already have!"

"All right!" David said. "Just making sure!"

After dinner Kathleen went back to her computer and pulled up the photo of the shire. He was still not adopted.

"Earnestly Seeking Galileo," she said. "You have *got* to find another home!"

Two days later, the new foals arrived. They came late in the morning, and Kathleen left work early to get home in time to help unload. It was a completely different scene from when Benny, Bart and Beatrice arrived.

Foals number B-7 and B-14 were wild. They exited the trailer like bucking broncos coming out of the chute, wild-eyed, kicking, lunging, tossing their heads, and worst of all, both of them were determined to jump the fence and escape. The driver stayed to help Kathleen and Cathy corral them into the smaller pen to try to calm them down, but the foals wanted nothing to do with them. They tore around the paddock, tossing huge chunks of dirt and grass into the air. If anyone got near them they tried to jump the fence. To everyone's surprise, they could almost make it over.

"We have to get them in the little pen before they get hurt," Kathleen said, breathless, as the chestnut left another huge dent in the top rail of the fence.

"We have to get them in before *we* get hurt!" Cathy said.

They each got a horse blanket and held them out at arms length to make a wall and slowly managed to push the babies in the right direction. Several times one of them lunged through a tiny space between the blankets and took off towards the other side of the paddock and each time Kathleen and Cathy started again and quietly backed them towards the gate.

Finally, when their arms were tired and aching from holding the blankets and their eyes burned from the salty sweat dripping into them, they managed to get the colts into the pen and slam the door. The foals immediately tried to jump the fence, over and over again, but because the pen was so small, they couldn't run far enough to get the speed they needed to hurdle over. Their captors moved away from them and the horses finally calmed down.

"Wow!" Kathleen said. "What in the world do we have here?"

"I don't know," Cathy said, watching a small flock of crows take off from the roof of the barn and fly towards the farmhouse, "but I think we have a lot of work ahead of us."

Wilson and Carl swooped in and landed on the fence alongside the foals' paddock.

"Dudes! You should have seen what we just saw!" Wilson said. "Holy cow! Those new foals are insane, dudes! Like, wild horses!"

"Like, *really* wild horses!" Carl said. "They're trying to break the fences down over there!"

Cressida rolled her eyes. "It's been done," she said. "No big deal."

"No, man," Wilson said. "They're nuts! I don't know what's wrong with them, but they're crazy!"

Carla landed beside the boys.

"Well, I have never seen such a display of bad behavior in all my life!" she said. "They are a disgrace to horses everywhere!"

"They sound like their really cool!" Bart said, trying to see past the big barn.

"What's the matter with them?" Calypso asked.

"Well, first of all, they need a good, swift kick to their backsides!" Carla said. "I asked them what their problem was and they were exceptionally rude! It turns out they've been running wild for the past few months with no adult horses and no humans to teach them any manners. These two, it seems, were the closest thing to leaders those other babies had up north. Talk about setting a bad example! And we were lucky enough to get them here! Hmmph!"

"Wow!" Carl said. "So, they're like gang leaders? Cool!"

"How many times have I warned you about getting involved with gangs?" Carla said. "They will ruin your lives! You two stay away from that barn until those horses either calm down or go away, do you hear me?"

"Yes, mother," Carl said.

"Wilson, do you hear me?"

"Yes, Carla," Wilson said.

Carla flew off towards the pine tree.

"Your mother is tough," Wilson said. "She never gets tired, does she?"

"She hasn't yet," Carl said, and the two of them flew after her.

"Mama, what's a gang?" Ezzie asked Doc.

"Nothing you'll ever have to worry about here," Doc said, then muttered, "I hope!"

Duck came waddling into the paddock.

"Hey! How'd you get out?" Cressida asked.

"Kathleen came home and shut the gate but didn't latch it," Duck replied. "Wow, was she in a bad mood!"

"The new foals are gang members," Ezzie said.

"No, they are not," Cressida said. "You can't have a gang with just two members."

"But it sounds like they're going to be a lot of trouble," Classy said.

"Well, then, Locket, I think you and I should go right on over and straighten them out!" Duck said, grinning and wagging his tail. "I've been pretty bored, lately, you know."

"No, thank you," Locket said. "My traveling days are over for good. I'm staying right here in this paddock."

Cathy came over from the barn to get Calypso for lessons, and as she led her through the gate, Classy called out to the old pony, "Find out what you can!"

"I can't wait to see these two," Calypso called back over her shoulder. "They'll have a rude awakening. Kathleen's never going to put up with all that nonsense."

Cathy led Calypso inside the big barn to get her ready for her lesson so she didn't have a chance to see the new foals right away. It was Ethan's lesson day and she decided he was going to get more of a ride than usual.

The lesson started in the outdoor ring and Calypso could see the two new foals from where she trotted at a nice, even pace. One of them was a chestnut with a star on his forehead and the other a dun appaloosa with a spotted blanket on his butt. The two of them were busily eating hay while still keeping a close eye on what was happening on the farm. Calypso thought the chestnut made a face at her when he caught her looking at him.

At the end of each lesson Cathy took her students up to the back field for a canter. She, Calypso and Ethan walked up the long drive towards the log cabin, but when they reached the top, Calypso turned around and bolted down the hill.

"Hey! Hey!" Ethan shouted, grabbing a chunk of her mane to hang on.

Cathy started running after them, but her two legs were no match for Calypso's four.

"Hey!" Ethan shouted again and pulled back on the reins, but Calypso had gotten the bit between her teeth and there was nothing he could do to stop her.

They reached the bottom of the hill and Calypso raced around the corner to the foals' pen. The appaloosa snorted at her, and the chestnut burst out laughing.

"Ha! What do you have on your back, old lady?" he said.

"It's a child," Calypso said.

"Throw if off!" The chestnut snorted.

"What is your problem?" Calypso asked, while Ethan tried to get his foot back into the stirrup he'd lost during their run downhill.

"Problem? I don't have a problem," the chestnut said. "Anybody here got a problem?" he asked looking at the appaloosa, who shook his head. "Nope, looks like the only one here with a problem is you, and you can't get him off you back!"

The two foals burst out laughing.

"If I were your mother, I'd . . ." Calypso started.

"But you're not," the appaloosa said. "We don't have mothers. They left us – took off with some farmer who they must have liked a lot better than they liked us."

"Well, I know that is certainly *not* true!" Calypso said. "And you should know it, as well!"

"What do you know?" the chestnut said. "You weren't there!"

Calypso wanted to explain about their mothers, but she'd run out of time.

"There you are!" Cathy said as she came around the corner of the barn. "Calypso, what has gotten into you? That's twice you've taken off, now! All right, Ethan, good job of staying on."

"It was fun!" Ethan said. "Can I do it again?"

"No," Cathy replied. "Let's finish up in the indoor arena, OK?"

She took Calypso's reins and led her away, but not before she heard the appaloosa mutter, "What does she care? I'm not gonna be staying here, anyway."

Kathleen was in the house at her computer trying to think of a topic for her weekly newspaper column. She'd started to write it twice, but each time she decided she didn't like it and erased it. She'd already called David on the phone and told him the story of the wild foals in the quarantine paddock and he had laughed and said he was sure she'd figure out how to tame them.

"I don't know," Kathleen said. "They're a lot bigger than the other ones were when we got them. They can almost jump the fence!"

"So that means we have some champion event horses on our farm!" David said.

"I don't know about that," she said, "but I do know these guys make Beatrice look like a newborn lamb."

"We can handle them," David said before he hung up.

Kathleen gave up trying to write. Instead, she typed in the foal adoption website and pulled up the photo of the appaloosa. It was taken when he was only a few days old and he looked like such a sweet baby in his photo. What happened to make him so crazy? She stared at it for a few minutes before she heard the familiar voice ringing in her head.

"Earnestly Seeking Galileo," she said, clicking over to his photo. He was still not adopted. "Why are you doing this to me?"

Chapter Eighteen

Solitary confinement

David stood at the counter in Dick Farrell's feed and supply store.

"What's the strongest metal fence you have?" he asked.

"The one I sold you a few weeks ago," Dick replied. "It's supposed to be strong enough to keep buffalo in."

"Not strong enough for these guys, and they aren't buffalo!" David said. "Well, do you have anything taller?"

"Taller than five feet?" Dick asked, amazed. "There ain't nothin' gonna get over five foot fence. What do you got over there? Kangaroos?"

"We've got two little foals with more spunk than anything I've ever seen," David said. "They've dented up all the fencing we have and they're coming real close to being able to jump over it."

"Geez, David," Dick said. "Why are you still messin' with those PMU babies? I got a couple of nice, quiet, older horses just perfect for you and your wife. Give 'em to ya at a good price, too!"

"Dick, do you know my wife at all?"

"Right," Dick replied. "Well, good luck to ya, then!"

"Oh, throw in a few extra lead ropes, too," David said. "I have a feeling we'll be breaking a few before these guys are tamed."

"Need any more halters?" Dick asked.

"Nope!" David said. "We have plenty of those. Kathleen's at home trying to get them on those guys right now."

"They didn't come with halters?" Dick asked, amazed.

"It seems they were running wild in the pastures up north," David said, "and it's not safe to turn them out with halters on."

Dick shook his head and whistled between his teeth.

"She's a crazy one, that wife of yours," he said.

Kathleen sat on a bale of hay in the foals' pen. It had been a week since they'd arrived, and she'd made little progress. She still couldn't get near the foals without them going crazy and throwing themselves into the fencing, so she sat in the pen on a bale of hay and moved as little as possible, hoping they would eventually get used to her and approach her for food the way the other babies had.

Kathleen had named the appaloosa Bingo, and Brendee, who had adopted the chestnut, decided to call him Star. Kathleen liked to call them the Killer Colts. She'd already been kicked in the chest by Star, and while she was pretty sure he had fractured one of her ribs, she kept quiet about it. She'd also been slammed into the barn wall by Bingo and broken a finger, but it wasn't so bad she needed to wear a splint on it so she kept quiet about that, as well. David didn't need to know she was getting clobbered in the paddock. After her success with Beatrice he had decided she could handle the wildest of babies and seldom asked how she was doing with them. Had he asked, however, the answer wouldn't have been very positive. Kathleen had never before worked so hard to stay patient.

"They're only babies," she told herself over and over again. "They don't know what they're doing because no one ever taught them manners. It's my job to teach them manners."

Kathleen decided the foals had to be separated and put in stalls inside the barn so they would stop encouraging each other to be bad but she didn't dare try to get them inside until she got halters on them. If they ever got loose without halters it would take forever to catch them. Kathleen still hadn't been able to get close to them. The only thing she'd had success with is getting them to like grain and she was convinced she could use food to lure them close enough to get halters over their faces.

She sat on a hay bale with a halter dangling in a bucket of grain. If a foal stuck his head in the bucket to eat she planned to pull the halter up over his nose and snap it closed. It was chilly outside and Kathleen's hands were cold, but she knew if she had gloves on she'd never be able to fasten the clip quickly enough.

"Come on, Killers," she said, softly and sweetly. "Come see momma, pretty babies, and I'll give you a nice snack."

She shook the bucket so they could hear the grain rattling around. She knew they were hungry because she'd been sitting on their bale of hay for more than an hour and they hadn't gone near it since she'd gotten there.

"Come on, little monsters," she cooed. "It's delicious!"

Kathleen picked up a handful and held it out towards them. Her hand was shaking and turning blue from the cold, but the foals were showing some interest. Bingo was the first to slowly walk towards her. She let the grain drop back into the bucket from her outstretched hand.

"Work for it, you lovely little beast!" she said, smiling. "Walk that pretty spotted butt right over here."

Slowly, slowly, Bingo came closer. He stretched his neck

towards the bucket and dipped his face in, then pulled back quickly.

"Wimp," Kathleen said, as sweetly as she could. "Can't do it, can you?"

Bingo stretched closer and reached his face in again. Kathleen didn't move. She wanted to wait until he was so busy eating his grain he didn't notice what she was doing. His mouth was getting closer to the noseband of the halter, but she waited until he was in the perfect position. She slowly lifted the band, and just as he realized there was something slipping over his head, she yanked it right over his ears. Bingo leaped back and bucked around the pen, sending the bucket flying, and Kathleen flattened herself against the barn wall. She'd gotten kicked enough times to know not to chase him. Bingo tossed his head from side to side, desperate to get the halter off his face, but luck was with Kathleen and it stayed on.

"I am the foal goddess!" she said and settled back on the hay bale with her bucket.

The next time he came for grain, she'd hook the halter closed.

Two days later, Kathleen had finally gotten halters on both foals. She'd also gotten a black eye from when she'd finally hooked Star's halter closed and he swung his face out of the bucket

145

and smack into hers.

It was time to put them in solitary confinement. She and Cathy took sections of metal fence and made an enclosed path from the back paddock all the way into the barn.

"Can't we just try to get them to lead?" Cathy asked.

"Not these two," Kathleen said, "unless you want to lose a few teeth."

"It just seems a little extreme to spend forty minutes putting up a fence to move them," Cathy said.

"For these guys, I don't think it would be extreme to wear a suit of armor!"

That night, the horses at the small barn could hear the foals screaming, crying and banging around in their stalls from all the way over in their paddock.

"They aren't so tough when they don't have each other," Calypso said. "So much for their little gang!"

The old pony was still feeling insulted from what the colts said to her when they first arrived.

"They'll come around," Beatrice said. "They'll get lonely and want to make friends."

"I hope they figure it out fast," Locket said. "I heard Kathleen say these guys are so tough, she isn't ever going to adopt another foal again. Somewhere out there, Ernie is trying to find his way here . . . and I'm afraid he may not have much time left."

Kathleen could also hear the foals making a fuss in the big barn, so she turned on the radio and turned the volume up high. She was tired. There was still so much work to do with the first three foals they had adopted but all of her time was going towards trying to get two very difficult babies under control, or at least get them to the point where they would stop hurting her.

She turned on the computer to check her email, and the name "Earnestly Seeking Galileo" popped into her head again.

"I can't!" she shouted at her computer. "Look at me! I'm tired! I'm bruised! How can I take another horse when I can't handle the ones I already have?"

Yet, she couldn't help herself. She clicked onto the foal adoption site, and there was the horse, still available with only four days left before he would be sent to a feed lot and then to slaughter.

"You don't understand!" she whispered. "I can't save every horse in the whole world!"

And the huge shire looked back at her from his photo and seemed to ask, "Why not?"

Chapter Nineteen

The foal moon

Locket was the only one awake at three o'clock in the morning. A late October moon, huge, round and orange, hung low in the eastern sky, and Locket wondered if it was the same moon her old friends in Death Valley were seeing that night. The air was chilly and her breath hung frosty and white around her face. Locket liked the cool weather best. Her coat was thick and warm and the vicious biting bugs of summer were long gone. The farm was quiet except for the sound of dry, brown leaves rustling as they gently landed on the ground.

"Locket? Locket, are you awake?"

It was Ernie. Locket had been expecting to hear from him.

"Hi, Ernie," she replied. "I'm awake."

"Do you know if I'm going to come there, yet?" he asked.

"I don't know, Ernie," she said. "I haven't heard anything. We're trying as hard as we can, but with humans . . . well, sometimes it can be hard to make them understand."

"Why?"

"They're really busy all the time," Locket said. "It makes it difficult for them to hear some really important things. And sometimes, they just don't trust their feelings, or they're afraid of them."

"They aren't afraid of me, are they?" Ernie said. "I know I'm very big, but . . ."

"No Ernie, these people would never be afraid of you," Locket said. "And as soon as you got here, they would love you very much."

"I hope so . . ."

"What's it like where you are?" Locket asked. "It's nice and cool outside where I am and the leaves are starting to fall off the trees. The stars are very bright tonight."

"It's like that here, too," Ernie said. "And the moon is rising. It's very bright and round."

"And orange?" asked Locket.

"Yes," Ernie replied.

"We're looking at the exact same moon at the exact same time!" Locket said.

They were both quiet for a few minutes while they shared the giant moon in the sky.

"You know, if I don't get there, it's OK," Ernie said. "I know I don't have very much time left, but I'm not afraid. I'm just happy we got to be friends. You're my best friend, Locket."

"You can't give up," Locket said.

"But it's not working," Ernie said. "I wish and wish and wish and it still doesn't work."

"Do you know about magic?" Locket asked.

"No," Ernie said. "What is it?"

"It's this feeling – a powerful feeling that's all around us," she said. "It makes dreams comes true, but only if you believe in it. If you stop believing in it, it can't work. Do you understand?"

"I think so," Ernie said.

"Look at the moon," Locket said. "I think if we both make a wish on the moon together, the exact same moon at the exact same time, maybe it will make the magic even stronger. Look at the moon right now and wish that you could come here to our meadow."

"Right now?"

"Right now!"

And the two of them, thousands of miles apart, wished as hard as they could.

They were quiet for a few minutes, then Ernie said, "I feel better."

"Me, too, Earnestly Seeking Galileo," Locket replied. "Why don't you try to get some sleep, now?"

"I will," Ernie said.

"Promise you won't stop believing?" Locket asked.

"I promise," Ernie said. "Good night, Locket."

"Good night, Ernie."

Locket took a deep breath and stared at the moon a little longer. Then she went inside the stall and woke Classy up.

"I just talked to Ernie," she said. "He doesn't have much longer."

"I know," Classy said and scrambled to her feet.

"Do you really think Kathleen knows about him?"

"I've done my best," Classy said.

"Come outside and see the moon," Locket said, and Classy followed her out into their pen.

"We wished on it tonight, Ernie and I," Locket said.

"It's a perfect wishing moon," Classy said. "I've made many wishes on the moon."

"Did they come true?" Locket asked.

"The most important one did," Classy said, "and it was a much

151

smaller moon than this one."

The two of them stared up at the moon together and wished one more time with all their hearts.

Kathleen was also awake. She'd just had a dream about something that had happened a long, long time ago. It was an early winter evening and she was at a theater watching people at a play rehearsal. A friend of hers told her she'd seen a very small kitten outside near the road and she was worried it would get hit by a car. Kathleen knew she should catch it and put it in her car, but she was married to someone else then, and that husband had told her she was not allowed to bring any more cats home. This time, she thought, someone else would have to be responsible for it. She turned back to watching the actors. A few minutes later, her friend came back inside and told her the kitten had been hit by a car and killed.

Kathleen hadn't thought about that kitten in a long time, even though when it had first happened it had changed her life forever. That was the day she learned never to expect someone else to take care of what she could take care of herself. While she never stopped blaming herself for the kitten's death, she knew that over the years she had saved many, many other animal because of what that kitten had taught her.

"Earnestly Seeking Galieo," said the familiar voice.

Then she heard it again, but this time is sounded like two

voices, then three. Kathleen got out of bed and turned on her computer. While it booted up, she wandered to the window and stared at the moon, which was huge and perfectly round and just dipping below the trees. She reached up and felt her eye where the swelling was finally going down from her most recent encounter with Star and Bingo. Her chest ached where she had been kicked, and her finger throbbed where it was broken.

"How much more do I have to do?" she asked the moon.

She went back to her computer and typed in the foal adoption website. She clicked on the picture of the shire, and it enlarged, filling the screen.

"You are not a kitten!" she said. "You are a giant horse! You take up a huge amount of room and you are very expensive to feed! I can't save every horse in the world!"

She looked at the words beneath him. Two days left, and he was still not adopted.

And the three voices said, "Just save this one."

Chapter Twenty

It takes a mommy

The next day was Saturday. Kathleen tossed handfuls of peanuts out the door to the waiting squirrels and crows then headed to the other door to throw softened dog food to the yard birds. David sat at the kitchen table reading the newspaper and drinking his second cup of coffee.

"I think we have to send Bingo and Star out for training," she said as she passed him.

"What?" David looked up from his paper. "What do you mean?"

He stood up and followed her to the other door. "What do you mean?" he asked again.

Kathleen stepped barefoot onto the cold walkway and tossed the food to the ducks, who came running from the pond.

"I mean they're too tough for me," Kathleen said. "I don't think I can handle those foals. I'm not sure I want to."

"Oh, no, no, no," David said. "You're just saying that for my sake, right? You're saying that because you think I would feel better if we had fewer horses here, right?"

"No, David, I'm saying it because I'm just really, really tired."

"But you're the one who insisted we had to keep Beatrice here!" David said. "What's so different about these two?"

"Star isn't ours," Kathleen said, "and we're not even going to keep Bingo!"

"Yeah, right," David said. "I never believed that for one second."

"These guys aren't like the others," she said. "They were older when they got here, and they ran wild for so long. I know they're frightened and angry, but it also seems like they just don't care about anything. I don't know if I can get through to them."

Duck grabbed hold of Kathleen's sweatpants and tugged and she reached down and moved him away.

"Behave and eat your breakfast, Duck," she said.

"Aren't your feet freezing?" David asked, looking down at her bare feet on the cement.

"Yes," Kathleen said. "Do you see those two crows? I think those same two crows stand on the fence every day waiting for the ducks to finish."

Duck tugged on her pants again.

"Hey! You stop that!" She said and moved him away again.

David held the door open and they went back inside.

"Here, put these on," David said reaching into the laundry basket and picking out a pair of thick socks. "My feet are cold just thinking about yours."

Kathleen sat in a kitchen chair and pulled the socks on, pausing to rub her lower back which had begun to ache from wrestling with the babies.

"I have an idea," David said. "How about you work with the first three foals and I'll take on Bingo and Star as my own project?"

Kathleen looked up from her second sock.

"You have never trained a foal in your life!" she said.

"I can figure it out," he said. "I've watched you and I . . . I can read books!"

"You are serious," Kathleen said slowly.

"Why not?"

"Well, you just go ahead and do that," Kathleen said, "but I suggest you wear a helmet and padded clothing, 'cause these guys can kick!"

She stood up and got an ice bag from the freezer and tucked it into the back of her jeans where her spine ached the most. Then she took two aspirin and grabbed a jacket.

"I'm going to work with Beatrice, Bart and Benny," she said. "You do whatever you like!" And she walked outside.

Wilson and Carl, who had been sitting on the fence waiting for breakfast, overheard the conversation David and Kathleen had outside the back door.

"Those foals are in big trouble, dude," he said. "Someone should tell them to chill before they end up, like, gone!"

"They aren't very smart, if you ask me," Carl said, then flapped his wings and took off.

"You didn't even eat yet, dude!" Wilson called after him. "Where ya goin?"

"I gotta go talk to my mother!" Carl called back and Wilson flew after him.

"I knew they'd come to a bad end," Carla said after the boys told her their story. "It's just not safe to be away from Locket's Meadow. How foolish of them!"

"What are you gonna do, Ma?" Carl asked.

Wilson looked from one of them to the other and thought,

"Wassup with this?" He had never seen anyplace like this in his entire short life. Everyone here was always trying to *do* something to help someone else.

"Well, I don't know for sure, but I'm going to go talk to the horses," Carla said, and she took off with the boys flying close behind her.

"Wow," Calypso said when Carla told them the news. "Well, it's not like they didn't ask for it."

"There isn't much we can do about it," Classy said. "Every single gate and stall is double locked since the 'great flying burro escape.'"

"I'm afraid we're out of chances," Locket said.

Duck strutted into the paddock.

"How'd you get out this time?" Cressida asked.

"I broke a picket off the fence," he said. "I should have broken two. I almost got stuck squeezing through."

"Been there, done that," Cressida said.

"Did you hear about the foals?" Duck asked.

"Yes," Cressida said. "Not much we can do about it."

"I can go over there and talk to them," Duck said. "It's daylight."

"No, you can't," Locket said. "Those foxes are out during the day. You stay right here."

"Well, I know what to do," Carla said. "This is a job for a

mother. Boys, you wait here until I get back!"

"Cool, dude!" Wilson said. "Someone's gonna get in trouble, and it isn't even us!"

Kathleen walked outside and headed for the barn. Three crows were lined up on the fence between the girls' and the foals' paddock and all the horses were crowded around as if they were listening to them tell a fascinating story. One of the crows flew away towards the big barn and all the animals turned to watch her go. Then she saw Duck standing between the two goats.

"Duck!" she yelled. "What are you doing! You get back in your yard right now!"

Duck hung his head and waddled back towards the yard.

"How does he keep doing that?" Kathleen muttered.

She let him into the yard then went into the barn and grabbed a halter and a lead rope.

"Miss Bea!" she called. "You're first!"

Beatrice hesitated before leaving the group, then trotted over to Kathleen and dipped her head so she could slip the halter on easily.

The first three foals were all doing so well, Kathleen thought. Beatrice was leading beautifully and had already learned voice commands for walk, trot and stop. The filly loved attention, and most of all, she loved it when Kathleen kissed her on the nose.

Benny was learning almost as quickly. He led well most of the time and worked very hard at understanding what Kathleen wanted him to do. He wasn't very tall or strong or athletic, but he was willing to learn and very good-natured.

Bart was a little slower than the others and sometimes forgot exactly what it took to put one foot in front of the other and go forward when he was asked, but he was sweet and affectionate so no one minded. And he was so handsome! His coat was as bright and shiny and red as a brand new copper penny.

It was a nice, clear, cool fall day, and Beatrice willingly followed Kathleen as she walked up the hill towards the back fields.

David watched them through the kitchen window.

"How hard could it be?" he said.

The shelves in the living room were filled with books about training horses and David chose a few and sat at the kitchen table to read. He thumbed through one, but didn't see anything he thought would be useful. The second one was even less helpful. What did "ground yielding" mean, anyway? He tossed it onto the table and got his jacket.

"How hard can this be?" he asked again then grabbed his hat and went outside.

Carla had never flown into the big barn before. She didn't like enclosed spaces and there was always the threat of the barn cat. However, she was so angry, she couldn't stop herself.

She swept through the open doorway, startling some barn swallows who had never seen a crow invade their territory before.

"Excuse me," Carla said, "so sorry. I didn't mean to scare anyone."

She glanced into the stalls as she flew past. When she found Bingo and Star in adjoining stalls she landed on the edge of a trash can in the wash stall directly across from the two wild foals.

"Oh, look," said Bingo. "It's that nagging old bird."

"Back off, old lady," Star said. "No authority figures allowed here."

They snickered, but Carla could see they'd lost some of their spirit. Solitary confinement was taking its toll.

"All right, young men," Carla said. "It's time for you to hear a story. You're going to learn the truth about your mothers and what would have happened to you if you hadn't come to Locket's Meadow, even if it kills me!"

The barn cat came slinking out of the feed room, eyes focused on Carla.

"Back off, Fluffy!" Carla screamed at her. "I have no patience for you, today!"

Carla screeched a mighty caw at her and the cat was so startled she fled straight out the barn doors. The foals were also surprised and each took a step backwards.

"Now, you listen to me and you listen to me good," Carla began, and the foals stood, mouths open, too stunned to say a word.

Twenty minutes later, David walked into the barn. He ducked as a large crow flew over his head and out the door.

"Odd," he muttered, then ducked again as a small flock of barn swallows flew back into the barn.

He found Bingo and Star backed into the corners of their stalls and looking dazed.

"Hey, are you two OK?" David asked. "What's the matter, Bingo? Ghosts?"

Bingo walked towards David and stuck his nose between the bars of the stall. David slowly reached out and gently rubbed it.

"Now, how hard can this be?" David said. "I don't know what Kathleen's talking about."

An hour later, Kathleen was leading Bart down the hill when she saw David leading Star out of the barn.

"Oh, no," she said. "He's lost his mind."

She tried to hurry down, but Bart was having trouble remembering how to walk.

"One foot in front of the other, Bart!" she urged. "Come on!"

"What are you doing?" she called to David when she finally

got closer. "Are you crazy? He'll kill you! And you'll never catch him if he gets loose!"

"No, he's fine," David called back. "He's not even pulling on the rope!"

Kathleen got a little closer, but not too close. She had too many reminders of the pain the little horse could inflict.

David slowly walked the foal around the driveway, and while Star willingly followed, he seemed frightened to Kathleen.

"All right, what did you do to him?" Kathleen asked. "How did you get him to do this?"

"Well," David answered, "sometimes . . . it just takes . . . a daddy."

Late that night Kathleen sat at the kitchen table watching the glow of the moon through the window. It had been such a long day and she was tired, but she couldn't sleep. She kept hearing that name, over and over, and she was afraid if she fell asleep, she'd dream of the kitten again . . . or worse.

She threw a jacket on over her T-shirt and slipped into her boots.

The barn was dark except for a tiny night light and Kathleen walked down the aisle, listening to the breathing of sleeping animals. She inhaled the scent of horses and hay and cold, clean air, then slipped out the other end of the barn and was surprised to see both Classy and Locket standing outside their stall, staring at the moon.

"What are you two girls doing awake this late?" she whispered.

They turned to look at her for a moment, and Classy nickered a brief hello before they both turned back to staring at the moon. Kathleen followed their gaze.

"You two look like you're making a wish," she said.

Kathleen stood staring at the moon with them for a few minutes longer. Then she went into the house and turned on the computer. The photo of Ernie came up quickly, and beneath it were the words, "Last chance to adopt this foal is today."

It was 4 o'clock in the morning and there was something she had to do or she might never be able to sleep again.

Chapter Twenty-One

The homecoming

It had snowed for two days and fluffy white mounds blanketed the farm. In the dark, the pastures looked like a rolling, white ocean with its waves frozen into place. Snow clung thickly to the dark branches and the reflection of the moonlight made it look like millions of diamonds had dripped from the sky and settled in the trees.

The foals were in their pasture. They'd eaten plenty of hay in their warm shed and had come out to romp through the drifts and gaze at the moon.

Ernie had arrived weeks ago with the first snowfall. The truck driver had backed the horse trailer up to the barn and Ernie walked off the ramp, down the aisle and into his stall as if he had done it a thousand times. David and Kathleen had not expected that. They thought that an older foal would act more like Bingo and Star and they had prepared for the worst.

Ernie, however, had poked his nose over his stall door and let them touch his face right away, and they had stood outside his stall and stared at him in amazement. He was already as large as many of their full-grown horses and he seemed as wise as their old mares. It was hard to believe he would only be a year old in the spring. They'd have been surprised to learn he'd been coached by a burro whose wisdom ran as deep as any ocean.

A few weeks later, Ernie had his hernia surgery. He came home and rested in the boarder barn for a few more weeks before he was turned out to pasture with the other foals. There, he finally met his old friend Locket for the first time. There was no need for words – they already knew each other as well as they knew themselves. Locket reached up over her side of the fence and he leaned down. Their noses touched, and the two of them smiled.

The foals romped in the snow while Locket and Classy watched from their pen and Cressida watched through a crack in her stall wall. The Arab and the burro couldn't help but look at

Ernie, so tall, dark and handsome, while Cressida only had eyes for Beatrice, and those blue eyes of hers shone with tremendous pride.

Star was talking to Ernie, and the ladies watching from the barn could hear them clearly.

"Ernie," Star asked, "do you think my mommy can see the moon right now?"

The rest of the foals stopped romping and turned to hear his answer.

Kathleen was awake in the house. She usually could sleep very well, but tonight the sky was so bright, a crack of light peeked through the blinds and woke her. She looked through the window at the moon and saw all six foals standing in the pasture gazing at the sky and she gazed right along with them. It was as perfect a picture as any she had ever seen and she felt peaceful and happy as she watched them bathed in moonlight.

Out in the pasture, Ernie only hesitated a moment before he answered Star's question.

"I think all of our mommies can see this moon tonight," Ernie said.

All six foals turned their faces towards the moon and smiled.

And from where she watched in her stall, Cressida smiled, too.

About The Author

Kathleen M. Schurman, a journalist and playwright, lives at Locket's Meadow in Connecticut with her husband, David Melina, and dozens of animal friends, most of them rescues. She is on the board of directors of Foal Adoption Network, Inc. (FANI) and Foal Aid Support Team (FASTeam, Inc). Much of her time is spent listening as the animals tell their stories, then writing them down so everyone can hear their voices. A percentage of all sales of this book go towards horse rescue projects through the above-named charities.

About the illustrator

Catherine W. Hamill is a professional artist who lives and paints in Milford, Connecticut. She is active in the Milford Fine Arts Council and is the manager of the Firehouse Gallery at Walnut Beach Village. Catherine's paintings are exhibited throughout the world, and she is best known for capturing the spirit of a scene, a moment, or a gentle burro with a big heart.

Printed in the United States
16029LVS00002BA/85-254